I0007656

The Cybersecurity Bible

The Ultimate Guide to Mastering IT Security with Proven Training Techniques, Certification Strategies, and Expert Insights +500 Quizzes to Prepare Your Industry Certification Exam

Friedrich Haus

© **Copyright 2024 FRIEDRICH HAUS all rights reserved**

This document is geared towards providing exact and reliable information with regard to the topic and issue covered. The publication is sold with the idea that the publisher is not required to render accounting, officially permitted, or otherwise qualified services. If advice is necessary, legal or professional, a practiced individual in the profession should be ordered.

From a Declaration of Principles which was accepted and approved equally by a Committee of the American Bar Association and a Committee of Publishers and Associations.

In no way is it legal to reproduce, duplicate, or transmit any part of this document in either electronic means or in printed format. Recording of this publication is strictly prohibited, and any storage of this document is not allowed unless with written permission from the publisher. All rights reserved.

The information provided herein is stated to be truthful and consistent, in that any liability, in terms of inattention or otherwise, by any usage or abuse of any policies, processes, or directions contained within is the solitary and utter responsibility of the recipient reader. Under no circumstances will any legal responsibility or blame be held against the publisher for any reparation, damages, or monetary loss due to the information herein, either directly or indirectly.

Contents

List of Acronyms

1. **ACL** - Access Control List: Defines permissions for resources on a network.

2. **AES** - Advanced Encryption Standard: Symmetric encryption algorithm for securing data.

3. **APT** - Advanced Persistent Threat: Long-term, targeted cyber attack.

4. **API** - Application Programming Interface: Set of rules for software interaction.

5. **ASLR** - Address Space Layout Randomization: Security technique to prevent exploit attacks.

6. **BGP** - Border Gateway Protocol: Protocol for exchanging routing information on the internet.

7. **BYOD** - Bring Your Own Device: Policy allowing employees to use personal devices.

8. **CAC** - Common Access Card: Secure identification card for federal employees.

9. **CAPTCHA** - Completely Automated Public Turing test to tell Computers and Humans Apart: Challenge-response test to differentiate humans from bots.

10. **CBT** - Computer-Based Training: Educational training delivered via computer systems.

11. **CCTV** - Closed-Circuit Television: Surveillance camera system for monitoring and security.

12. **CIO** - Chief Information Officer: Executive responsible for IT strategy and operations.

13. **CIRT** - Cyber Incident Response Team: Team handling and responding to cybersecurity incidents.

14. **CISO** - Chief Information Security Officer: Executive overseeing an organization's information security.

15. **CISSP** - Certified Information Systems Security Professional: Certification for information security management.

16. **CMDB** - Configuration Management Database: Repository for managing IT assets and configurations.

17. **COBIT** - Control Objectives for Information and Related Technology: Framework for IT governance and management.

18. **CRC** - Cyclic Redundancy Check: Error-detecting code for data transmission integrity.

19. **CSIRT** - Computer Security Incident Response Team: Team specializing in responding to computer security incidents.

20. **CSO** - Chief Security Officer: Executive responsible for overall security strategy.

21. **CTF** - Capture The Flag: Cybersecurity competition involving solving security-related challenges.

22. **CTO** - Chief Technology Officer: Executive responsible for technological innovation and strategy.

23. **CVSS** - Common Vulnerability Scoring System: Standard for assessing the severity of security vulnerabilities.

24. **CVE** - Common Vulnerabilities and Exposures: List of publicly disclosed cybersecurity vulnerabilities.

25. **DDoS** - Distributed Denial of Service: Attack aiming to overwhelm services with traffic.

26. **DLP** - Data Loss Prevention: Technologies to protect sensitive data from unauthorized access.

27. **DNS** - Domain Name System: System translating domain names into IP addresses.

28. **DMZ** - Demilitarized Zone: Network segment that separates internal and external networks.

29. **DRP** - Disaster Recovery Plan: Strategy for recovering from significant IT disruptions.

30. **EAP** - Extensible Authentication Protocol: Framework for authentication methods in networks.

31. **ECC** - Elliptic Curve Cryptography: Encryption technique based on elliptic curve theory.

32. **EDR** - Endpoint Detection and Response: Security solution for monitoring and responding to threats.

33. **EFS** - Encrypted File System: Windows feature for encrypting files and folders.

34. **EMET** - Enhanced Mitigation Experience Toolkit: Microsoft tool for improving application security.

35. **FIPS** - Federal Information Processing Standards: Standards for federal information systems and data.

36. **FTP** - File Transfer Protocol: Protocol for transferring files over a network.

37. **GRC** - Governance, Risk Management, and Compliance: Framework for managing organizational governance and risks.

38. **HIDS** - Host-based Intrusion Detection System: Security system monitoring and analyzing host activities.

39. **HIPAA** - Health Insurance Portability and Accountability Act: U.S. law for protecting health information privacy.

40. **HIPS** - Host-based Intrusion Prevention System: Security system preventing intrusions at the host level.

41. **HMAC** - Hash-based Message Authentication Code: Algorithm for verifying message integrity and authenticity.

42. **IAM** - Identity and Access Management: Systems managing user identities and access rights.

43. **IDS** - Intrusion Detection System: System for detecting unauthorized access or anomalies.

44. **IEC** - International Electrotechnical Commission: Organization developing international standards for electrical technologies.

45. **IKE** - Internet Key Exchange: Protocol for secure key exchange in IPsec.

46. **IoC** - Indicator of Compromise: Evidence that indicates a potential security breach.

47. **IoT** - Internet of Things: Network of interconnected devices and systems.

48. **IPSec** - Internet Protocol Security: Suite of protocols for securing internet communications.

49. **IRP** - Incident Response Plan: Procedures for handling and mitigating security incidents.

50. **ISMS** - Information Security Management System: Framework for managing information security risks.

51. **ISO** - International Organization for Standardization: Body developing and publishing international standards.

52. **ISP** - Internet Service Provider: Company providing internet access services.

53. **ITIL** - Information Technology Infrastructure Library: Framework for managing IT services and operations.

54. **KPI** - Key Performance Indicator: Metric used to evaluate success or performance.

55. **KVM** - Keyboard, Video, and Mouse: Device for controlling multiple computers from one set.

56. **L2TP** - Layer 2 Tunneling Protocol: Protocol for creating virtual private networks.

57. **LDAP** - Lightweight Directory Access Protocol: Protocol for accessing and maintaining directory information.

58. **MAC** - Mandatory Access Control: Access control policy where permissions are enforced by the system.

59. **MFA** - Multi-Factor Authentication: Security process requiring multiple forms of verification.

60. **MITM** - Man-In-The-Middle: Attack where an adversary intercepts communications between two parties.

61. **MPLS** - Multi-Protocol Label Switching: Technique for routing data in high-performance networks.

62. **MSP** - Managed Service Provider: Company providing outsourced IT services.

63. **MTBF** - Mean Time Between Failures: Average time

between system failures.

64. **MTTR** - Mean Time to Repair: Average time required to fix a system issue.

65. **NAC** - Network Access Control: System enforcing security policies on network access.

66. **NAT** - Network Address Translation: Technique for modifying network address information in packets.

67. **NIST** - National Institute of Standards and Technology: U.S. agency developing security standards and guidelines.

68. **OCTAVE** - Operationally Critical Threat, Asset, and Vulnerability Evaluation: Risk assessment methodology for organizations.

69. **OSI** - Open Systems Interconnection: Reference model for understanding network protocols.

70. **PaaS** - Platform as a Service: Cloud computing model providing a platform for developing applications.

71. **PCI-DSS** - Payment Card Industry Data Security Standard: Standards for securing payment card information.

72. **PKI** - Public Key Infrastructure: System managing digital keys and certificates.

73. **RAT** - Remote Access Trojan: Malware allowing remote control of an infected system.

74. **RBAC** - Role-Based Access Control: Access control policy based on user roles.

75. **RDP** - Remote Desktop Protocol: Protocol for accessing and managing computers remotely.

76. **RTO** - Recovery Time Objective: Target time for resuming critical functions after a disruption.

77. **RPO** - Recovery Point Objective: Maximum acceptable amount of data loss measured in time.

78. **SIEM** - Security Information and Event Management: System for collecting and analyzing security data.

79. **SLA** - Service Level Agreement: Contract defining the level of service expected from a provider.

80. **SOC** - Security Operations Center: Facility for monitoring and responding to security incidents.

81. **SOP** - Standard Operating Procedure: Document outlining procedures for consistent operations.

82. **SSH** - Secure Shell: Protocol for secure remote command-line access.

83. **SSL** - Secure Sockets Layer: Protocol for securing internet communications (predecessor to TLS).

84. **TLS** - Transport Layer Security: Protocol for encrypting data sent over networks.

85. **UEBA** - User and Entity Behavior Analytics: Security approach using behavior analytics to detect anomalies.

86. **URL** - Uniform Resource Locator: Address used to access resources on the internet.

87. **VPN** - Virtual Private Network: Service creating a secure connection over a public network.

88. **WAF** - Web Application Firewall: Security system filtering and monitoring HTTP traffic.

89. **WPA** - Wi-Fi Protected Access: Security protocol for wireless networks.

90. **XSS** - Cross-Site Scripting: Attack injecting malicious scripts into web pages.

91. **Zero Trust** - Security model assuming no trust and verifying every access request.

92. **IoT** - Internet of Things: Network of interconnected devices with unique identifiers.

93. **RAT** - Remote Access Trojan: Malware allowing remote access and control of infected systems.

94. **HIDS** - Host-based Intrusion Detection System: System monitoring and analyzing activities on hosts.

95. **CISO** - Chief Information Security Officer: Executive responsible for an organization's cybersecurity strategy.

96. **GRC** - Governance, Risk Management, and Compliance: Framework for managing organizational governance and risks.

97. **VLAN** - Virtual Local Area Network: Network segmentation within a physical network.

98. **MFA** - Multi-Factor Authentication: Security process requiring multiple forms of verification.

99. **DLP** - Data Loss Prevention: Technologies to protect sensitive data from unauthorized access.

100. **EPP** - Endpoint Protection Platform: Comprehensive solution for securing endpoints.

101. **NAC** - Network Access Control: System enforcing security policies on network access.

102. **CSRF** - Cross-Site Request Forgery: Attack exploiting the trust between a user and a website.

103. **SAML** - Security Assertion Markup Language: XML-based protocol for exchanging authentication and authorization data.

104. **NAT** - Network Address Translation: Technique for modifying network address information in packets.

105. **EIDAS** - Electronic Identification, Authentication and Trust Services: EU regulation for electronic transactions.

106. **RMS** - Risk Management System: System for identifying, assessing, and mitigating risks.

107. **GPG** - GNU Privacy Guard: Free implementation of the OpenPGP standard for encryption.

108. **SSO** - Single Sign-On: Authentication process allowing access to multiple applications with one login.

109. **BIA** - Business Impact Analysis: Process identifying critical functions and their impact on the organization.

110. **FIM** - File Integrity Monitoring: Monitoring changes to files to detect unauthorized modifications.

111. **CCPA** - California Consumer Privacy Act: California law providing consumer data protection rights.

112. **CMMC** - Cybersecurity Maturity Model Certification: Framework for cybersecurity maturity in defense contracting.

113. **OCSP** - Online Certificate Status Protocol: Protocol for checking the status of digital certificates.

114. **CPE** - Continuing Professional Education: Ongoing learning to maintain professional certifications.

115. **SIEM** - Security Information and Event Management: System for collecting and analyzing security-related data.

116. **CSP** - Cloud Service Provider: Company providing cloud computing services.

117. **CVE** - Common Vulnerabilities and Exposures: List of publicly disclosed cybersecurity vulnerabilities.

118. **CSPM** - Cloud Security Posture Management: Tools and practices for managing cloud security configurations.

119. **DNSSEC** - Domain Name System Security Extensions: Security extensions for DNS to protect against attacks.

120. **XDR** - Extended Detection and Response: Integrated security solution combining multiple detection tools.

121. **DAG** - Directed Acyclic Graph: Data structure used in various security contexts.

122. **PST** - Personal Storage Table: File format for storing Microsoft Outlook data.

123. **NIST** - National Institute of Standards and Technology: U.S. agency providing cybersecurity guidelines and standards.

124. **RDP** - Remote Desktop Protocol: Protocol for accessing and managing remote computers.

125. **IMSI** - International Mobile Subscriber Identity: Unique identifier for mobile network subscribers.

126. **TRM** - Trusted Resource Manager: System for managing trusted resources and security.

127. **OAUTH** - Open Authorization: Protocol for token-based authorization and access control.

128. **BPA** - Business Process Automation: Use of technology to automate business processes.

129. **VPN** - Virtual Private

Network: Service creating a secure, encrypted connection over the internet.

130. **POC** - Proof of Concept: Demonstration of feasibility or potential of a technology.

131. **QoS** - Quality of Service: Mechanisms for managing network traffic and performance.

132. **RAT** - Remote Access Tool: Software allowing remote control of a computer.

133. **SSP** - System Security Plan: Document detailing system security requirements and controls.

134. **VLAN** - Virtual Local Area Network: Logical network partition within a physical network.

135. **WPA2** - Wi-Fi Protected Access II: Enhanced security protocol for wireless networks.

136. **SYN** - Synchronize: TCP flag used during the handshake process of establishing connections.

137. **ZTA** - Zero Trust Architecture: Security model requiring verification for every network access request.

Introduction

What is the CompTIA Security+ Certification

The **CompTIA Security+** certification is a globally recognized credential that validates foundational skills in Cybersecurity. It serves as a benchmark for best practices in IT security and covers a wide range of topics including network security, threat management, cryptography, and risk management. This section provides an overview of what the certification entails and outlines the steps needed to achieve it.

CompTIA Security+ is an entry-level certification often regarded as the first step for professionals seeking to enter the field of cybersecurity. Designed for individuals with basic IT knowledge who aspire to specialize in security, this certification is vendor-neutral, meaning it covers general security concepts applicable across various platforms and technologies.

Key Domains Covered

The Security+ certification exam (SY0-701) is structured around five key domains:

1. **Threats, Attacks, and Vulnerabilities (24%)**: This domain covers various types of attacks such as phishing, malware, and ransomware. It also includes concepts related to vulnerability scanning, penetration testing, and social engineering techniques.

2. **Architecture and Design (21%)**: Focuses on secure network architecture, secure system design, cloud computing, and virtualization security. This domain emphasizes the importance of creating robust, secure infrastructures that can withstand various threats.

3. **Implementation (25%)**: This domain involves the implementation of secure protocols and services, configuring wireless security

settings, and deploying public key infrastructure (PKI). Practical aspects of applying security measures are the core focus here.

4. **Operations and Incident Response (16%)**: Covers incident response procedures, including how to handle and mitigate security incidents. It also delves into network and host-based security solutions, as well as digital forensics techniques to investigate breaches.

5. **Governance, Risk, and Compliance (14%)**: Focuses on the importance of adhering to governance, risk management, and compliance requirements. This includes understanding laws, regulations, and policies related to IT security.

The Winning Approach

Achieving the CompTIA Security+ certification involves several steps:

1. **Understand the Exam Objectives**: Review the official exam objectives provided by CompTIA to understand the scope of the exam. Familiarize yourself with each domain and the specific topics covered.

2. **Study and Prepare**: Use study materials such as textbooks, online courses, practice exams, and hands-on labs. Resources like the CompTIA CertMaster and other recognized study guides are valuable tools in your preparation.

3. **Gain Practical Experience**: While the Security+ is an entry-level certification, having hands-on experience with security tools and practices will greatly enhance your understanding and performance on the exam.

4. **Take Practice Exams**: Practice exams help you gauge your readiness and familiarize yourself with the exam format. Identify areas of weakness and focus your study efforts on those topics.

5. **Register for the Exam**: Once you feel confident in your knowledge and skills, register for the Security+ exam through the Pearson VUE platform. Select a test center or opt for an online proctored exam.

6. **Pass the Exam**: The Security+ exam consists of multiple-choice and performance-based questions. To pass, you need a score of 750 out of 900. Upon passing, you'll receive your certification and can proudly display your new credential.

Achieving the CompTIA Security+ certification is a significant step toward a successful career in cybersecurity. It not only validates your skills but also opens doors to advanced certifications and professional opportunities.

Topics Covered

The Security+ certification exam (SY0-701) is structured around five key domains, each encompassing a variety of topics critical to cybersecurity. Understanding these domains is essential for anyone preparing for the exam.

1. **Threats, Attacks, and Vulnerabilities (24%)**

    - **Types of Attacks**: This section covers various cyber threats such as phishing, spear phishing, malware, ransomware, and advanced persistent threats (APTs). It also discusses the techniques used by attackers to exploit vulnerabilities.
    - **Social Engineering**: Understanding the psychological manipulation techniques attackers use to trick individuals into divulging confidential information or performing actions that compromise security.
    - **Vulnerability Scanning and Penetration Testing**: This involves identifying vulnerabilities in systems and networks using tools and methodologies that mimic the techniques of attackers. The focus is on assessing security weaknesses and potential exploits.
    - **Threat Intelligence and Indicators of Compromise (IoC)**: Learning how to gather, analyze, and apply threat intelligence to identify signs of a security breach, such as unusual network activity or unauthorized access.

2. **Architecture and Design (21%)**

    - **Secure Network Architecture**: This topic covers the principles of designing and implementing secure networks, including the use of demilitarized zones (DMZs), segmentation, and secure communication channels.

- **Systems and Application Security**: Focuses on secure system configurations, hardening operating systems, and securing applications through secure coding practices and regular updates.
- **Cloud Security**: Addresses the unique challenges and security measures associated with cloud computing environments, including virtualization security and the shared responsibility model.
- **Virtualization and Container Security**: Explores how to secure virtual machines and containerized applications, ensuring isolation, integrity, and minimal attack surfaces.
- **Security Design Principles**: Covers the foundational principles of security design such as defense in depth, least privilege, and separation of duties.

3. **Implementation (25%)**

- **Secure Protocols and Services**: Understanding the implementation and configuration of secure communication protocols like HTTPS, TLS/SSL, IPsec, and SSH, which ensure data in transit is protected.
- **Identity and Access Management (IAM)**: Focuses on the tools and practices for managing user identities and access rights, including multi-factor authentication (MFA), single sign-on (SSO), and access control lists (ACLs).
- **Public Key Infrastructure (PKI)**: Involves the deployment and management of digital certificates, key pairs, and encryption technologies that support secure communications and data integrity.
- **Wireless Security Settings**: Discusses the security measures necessary for protecting wireless networks, including the use of WPA3, securing SSIDs, and implementing strong authentication protocols.
- **Endpoint Security**: Covers the implementation of security controls on devices such as computers, smartphones, and tablets, focusing on antivirus software, device encryption, and endpoint detection and response (EDR).

4. **Operations and Incident Response (16%)**

18

- **Incident Response Procedures**: Understanding the steps involved in responding to security incidents, including identification, containment, eradication, recovery, and lessons learned.
- **Disaster Recovery and Business Continuity Planning**: Focuses on the strategies and plans to ensure that critical business operations can continue or quickly resume following a disruptive incident.
- **Digital Forensics**: Involves the collection, preservation, analysis, and presentation of digital evidence in a manner suitable for use in legal proceedings. It includes understanding how to secure crime scenes and use forensic tools.
- **Mitigation Techniques**: Covers the practical approaches to mitigating the effects of cyber attacks, including patch management, network reconfiguration, and system restoration.
- **Logging and Monitoring Activities**: Understanding the importance of logging and monitoring systems to detect, respond to, and analyze security events and potential threats.

5. **Governance, Risk, and Compliance (14%)**

- **Security Policies and Procedures**: Understanding the creation and enforcement of security policies, procedures, and guidelines that align with organizational goals and regulatory requirements.
- **Risk Management**: Covers the process of identifying, assessing, and mitigating risks to information assets, including conducting risk assessments and implementing risk management frameworks.
- **Compliance Requirements**: Discusses the various laws, regulations, and industry standards that organizations must comply with, such as GDPR, HIPAA, and PCI-DSS, and the role of audits in ensuring compliance.
- **Security Awareness and Training**: Focuses on educating employees and stakeholders about cybersecurity risks, promoting best practices, and building a security-conscious culture within the organization.
- **Ethical Considerations in Cybersecurity**: Addresses the ethical responsibilities of cybersecurity professionals, including handling sensitive data, respecting privacy, and

conducting security activities within legal boundaries.

It might look "overwhelming", however considering the benefits of obtaining this certification might bring to your career, plus the fact that all the topics are well covered in this book you will no longer fear any of this!

Exam Format

The CompTIA Security+ certification exam (SY0-701) is designed to assess a candidate's foundational knowledge and skills in cybersecurity. Understanding the format of the exam is crucial for effective preparation. The exam includes a combination of question types that test both theoretical knowledge and practical problem-solving abilities.

Question Types

The Security+ exam features several types of questions to evaluate different aspects of cybersecurity expertise:

- **Multiple-Choice Questions (MCQs)**
- **Performance-Based Questions (PBQs)**
- **Drag-and-Drop Questions**
- **Fill-in-the-Blank Questions**

Exam Details

The CompTIA Security+ exam is structured to ensure a comprehensive assessment within a manageable timeframe:

- **Number of Questions**: The exam consists of a maximum of 90 questions, combining multiple-choice questions with performance-based tasks. The exact number may vary, but candidates can expect a mix of the different question types outlined above.
- **Time Limit**: Candidates are given 90 minutes to complete the exam. Time management is crucial, especially when tackling performance-based questions, which may require more time to solve than standard multiple-choice questions.
- **Passing Score**: The exam is scored on a scale from 100 to 900, with a passing score of 750. The scoring algorithm is proprietary to CompTIA, and not all questions carry the same weight, especially

the performance-based ones. This means that correct answers to more complex questions can potentially earn more points.

- **Exam Environment**: The exam can be taken at a Pearson VUE testing center or online with a remote proctor. Both environments require candidates to follow strict identification and security protocols to maintain the integrity of the certification process.

Scoring and Results

The scoring process for the CompTIA Security+ exam is designed to reflect the candidate's proficiency across various domains:

- **Weighted Scoring**: Not all questions are equal in value; some questions, especially performance-based ones, may contribute more significantly to the final score. CompTIA uses a complex scoring algorithm that takes into account the difficulty and type of questions.
- **Immediate Results**: Upon completion of the exam, candidates receive a provisional pass/fail result on-screen. The official score report, detailing performance in each domain, is usually available within a few hours via the candidate's CompTIA account.
- **Retake Policy**: If a candidate does not pass the exam, they must wait 14 days before retaking it. There is no limit to the number of retakes, but each attempt requires a new exam fee. Candidates are encouraged to review their performance and focus on weaker areas before retaking the exam.

Understanding the exam format helps candidates tailor their study strategies and manage their time effectively during the test. Familiarity with the types of questions and the structure of the exam can significantly improve performance and confidence.

Exam-Taking Skills

Success in the CompTIA Security+ exam not only depends on understanding the material but also on effective exam-taking skills. These skills help candidates manage their time, reduce anxiety, and maximize their performance during the test. Here are several strategies to consider:

Time Management

- **Pacing Yourself**: With 90 minutes to answer up to 90 questions, time management is crucial. Aim to spend an average of one minute per question. For performance-based questions, which may take longer, allocate more time, and compensate by moving quickly through easier multiple-choice questions.
- **Prioritizing Questions**: Start by answering the questions you find easiest. This approach helps build confidence and ensures you collect points early on. If a question seems too challenging or time-consuming, mark it for review and return to it later.
- **Keeping an Eye on the Clock**: Regularly check the timer, especially as you approach the halfway point of the exam. Ensure that you have enough time left to review marked questions and to carefully consider any performance-based tasks that require detailed work.

Handling Performance-Based Questions

- **Understanding the Scenario**: Performance-based questions (PBQs) often present a scenario where you must solve a problem in a simulated environment. Take a moment to fully understand the scenario before starting. Identify the key requirements and the tools available for solving the task.
- **Staying Calm Under Pressure**: PBQs can be complex and time-consuming. Approach them methodically, breaking down the tasks into smaller, manageable steps. If you feel stuck, move on and return later with a fresh perspective.
- **Practicing in Advance**: Familiarity with common cybersecurity tools and environments is crucial for PBQs. Practice using command-line tools, configuring network settings, and working through simulated scenarios to build your confidence and speed.

Reading and Interpreting Questions

- **Careful Reading**: Read each question thoroughly to avoid misinterpreting what is being asked. Pay attention to keywords such as "BEST," "MOST," or "LEAST," which can significantly change the meaning of the question.
- **Identifying Distractors**: Multiple-choice questions often include distractors—plausible but incorrect answers designed to confuse. Use the process of elimination to remove clearly wrong options and increase your chances of choosing the correct answer.
- **Answering the Question Asked**: Ensure that your answer directly

addresses the question. Avoid overthinking or adding information that is not provided in the question, as this can lead to incorrect assumptions and answers.

Dealing with Exam Anxiety

- **Preparing Thoroughly**: One of the best ways to reduce anxiety is thorough preparation. Familiarize yourself with the exam format, practice with sample questions, and ensure you understand the key concepts. The more prepared you are, the more confident you will feel.
- **Practicing Relaxation Techniques**: Before and during the exam, use relaxation techniques such as deep breathing, visualization, or mindfulness to stay calm. These techniques can help clear your mind and improve focus.
- **Taking Breaks If Needed**: If the exam environment allows, take a brief pause to collect your thoughts if you start feeling overwhelmed. Even a few seconds of closing your eyes and taking deep breaths can make a significant difference.

Reviewing and Double-Checking Answers

- **Marking for Review**: If you are unsure about an answer, use the "mark for review" feature to flag the question. This allows you to return to it later if you have time. Sometimes, a later question can trigger a memory or insight that helps you answer a previously difficult question.
- **Double-Checking Your Work**: If time permits, go back and review your answers, especially those you were uncertain about. Look for any misread questions or simple mistakes. However, avoid changing answers unless you are certain, as your first instinct is often correct.
- **Ensuring No Questions are Unanswered**: Leaving a question unanswered guarantees no points, so even if you are unsure, make an educated guess. There is no penalty for guessing on the Security+ exam, so it's better to take a chance than to leave a blank.

Simulating the Exam Environment

- **Practice Under Exam Conditions**: Simulate the exam environment by taking practice exams under timed conditions. This helps you get used to the pressure of the time limit and the format of the questions.

- **Familiarizing with the Testing Platform**: If you're taking the exam online or at a testing center, familiarize yourself with the testing platform's interface. Knowing how to navigate the system, flag questions, and use the available tools can save time and reduce stress during the actual exam.
- **Adapting to the Testing Environment**: Whether you are testing in a center or at home with remote proctoring, make sure your environment is comfortable and free of distractions. Ensure that your computer and internet connection meet the necessary requirements well before exam day.

Developing strong exam-taking skills can make a significant difference in your performance on the CompTIA Security+ exam. These strategies, combined with a solid understanding of the material, can help you approach the exam with confidence and increase your chances of success.

How to Access Your Free Video Courses

Included with any purchase of this volume there are some bonus materials!

You can access them by creating your private space inside our website. All you need to do is to scan the following QR Code or manually typing the link provided below.

To make things easy, just follow these steps:

1. Follow the link or Scan the QR Code:

Link: `www.testfly.space/welcome-cybersecurity`

QR Code:

2. Click the Button in the Welcome Page:

Once you scan the QR code you will be redirected to our Welcome Page. Inside this page you will see a button, click it to add to your cart in our store a FREE product containing your FREE video courses and materials.

3. Complete the FREE order:

Once you click the button you will be redirected to our checkout with the free product in the cart. Please insert Your data (Name and E-mail) to create your account and unlock the course.

4. Set your account and start to study:

After clicking "Place Your Order" in the checkout page your account will be created. You will see on the top of the page that the menu has been modified since now you are logged-in in our website.

All you need to do now is waiting for the email of confirmation with the link to reset your password.

Just do it for safety reason and log-in in your account by visiting www.testfly.space webiste.

Here you will always find all your materials and courses purchased within our webiste or books.

Well! It's all set. We can't wait to see you inside our interactive study platform!

Chapter 1: Cybersecurity 360

1.1 Importance of Cybersecurity

In today's digital age, cybersecurity has become an essential aspect of organizational strategy and operations. With the increasing reliance on digital technologies, interconnected systems, and the internet, protecting sensitive information from unauthorized access, theft, and compromise is crucial. Data breaches can lead to significant financial losses, legal consequences, and damage to reputation. Implementing robust cybersecurity measures helps safeguard personal data, financial records, intellectual property, and confidential business information, thereby maintaining trust and integrity.

Cybersecurity is also vital for maintaining business continuity. Cyber attacks, such as ransomware or denial-of-service (DoS) attacks, can disrupt operations, halt production, and result in substantial financial damage. By investing in strong cybersecurity practices, organizations can mitigate the risk of such disruptions and ensure that their operations remain functional and resilient. Effective cybersecurity practices are essential for avoiding operational downtime and ensuring that essential services continue without interruption.

Moreover, many industries are subject to stringent regulatory requirements concerning data protection and privacy. Regulations like the General Data Protection Regulation (GDPR), Health Insurance Portability and Accountability Act (HIPAA), and Payment Card Industry Data Security Standard (PCI-DSS) impose strict guidelines on handling and protecting sensitive data. Adhering to these regulations not only helps organizations avoid legal penalties but also builds credibility and trust with customers and stakeholders. Ensuring compliance with these standards further underscores the importance of cybersecurity in maintaining organizational integrity and public confidence.

1.2 History of Cybersecurity

The history of cybersecurity is a tale of evolving threats and increasingly sophisticated defenses. From its early beginnings in the 1970s to the present day, the field of cybersecurity has grown in complexity and importance, reflecting the rapid advancement of technology and the growing significance of digital information.

The origins of cybersecurity can be traced back to the 1970s when the concept of computer security was first formalized. In 1972, the United States Department of Defense developed the "DoD Trusted Computer System Evaluation Criteria," also known as the Orange Book. This document established foundational principles for evaluating the security of computer systems and marked the beginning of formal cybersecurity practices. During this period, the focus was primarily on protecting mainframe computers and their operating systems from unauthorized access and ensuring that data integrity was maintained.

The 1980s saw the advent of personal computing and networking, which introduced new challenges for cybersecurity. The development of the first computer viruses, such as the "Brain" virus in 1986, highlighted the need for antivirus software and protective measures. During this decade, the creation of the Computer Emergency Response Team (CERT) in 1988 by the Carnegie Mellon University further established the importance of responding to and managing cybersecurity incidents. The rise of computer networks also led to the creation of early firewalls and intrusion detection systems, setting the stage for more advanced security solutions.

The 1990s brought about significant advancements in cybersecurity with the proliferation of the internet and the World Wide Web. This era saw the introduction of various cybersecurity technologies, including encryption standards like the Secure Sockets Layer (SSL) protocol, which provided secure communication over the internet. The formation of the National Institute of Standards and Technology (NIST) in 1993 and the subsequent development of security frameworks and guidelines helped standardize cybersecurity practices across different sectors. Additionally, the emergence of new threats, such as email-based malware and phishing attacks, underscored the need for continuous innovation in security measures.

Entering the 2000s, cybersecurity faced unprecedented challenges due to the rapid expansion of online services and the increasing sophistication of cyber threats. The rise of advanced persistent threats (APTs) and complex malware demonstrated the need for more robust and adaptive security solutions. The establishment of industry standards like the Payment Card Industry Data Security Standard (PCI-DSS) and the introduction of comprehensive cybersecurity frameworks such as the NIST Cybersecurity Framework marked significant milestones in enhancing organizational security practices. The focus shifted toward holistic approaches that included threat intelligence, risk management, and incident response.

In recent years, the cybersecurity landscape has continued to evolve in response to emerging technologies and threats. The proliferation of cloud computing, the Internet of Things (IoT), and artificial intelligence (AI) has introduced new dimensions of risk and opportunity. Cybersecurity practices have adapted to these changes by incorporating advanced techniques such as machine learning for threat detection, zero-trust architectures, and automated response systems. The growing awareness of cybersecurity's importance has also led to increased regulatory requirements, industry certifications, and a focus on building a skilled cybersecurity workforce.

Overall, the history of cybersecurity reflects a dynamic and ongoing effort to protect digital assets in an increasingly interconnected world. As technology continues to advance, the field of cybersecurity will remain a critical component in ensuring the security and resilience of our digital infrastructure.

1.3 The Impact of a Cyberbreach in a Real Scenario

A cyberbreach can have far-reaching consequences for organizations, affecting various aspects of their operations, reputation, and financial stability. Understanding the potential impact of a cyberbreach is crucial for implementing effective security measures and preparing for potential incidents. Below are three scenarios illustrating the different ways a cyberbreach can impact an organization.

Scenario 1: WannaCry Ransomware Attack (2017)

In May 2017, the WannaCry ransomware attack affected over 200,000 computers across 150 countries. This global cyberattack exploited a vulnerability in Microsoft Windows known as EternalBlue, which was leaked by the Shadow Brokers group. WannaCry encrypted users' files and demanded ransom payments in Bitcoin.

Impact: - *Healthcare Disruption:* The UK's National Health Service (NHS) was particularly affected. Many hospitals had to cancel appointments and divert emergency patients because their systems were locked, leading to significant delays in patient care and operational disruptions. - *Financial Costs:* The estimated total damage from the WannaCry attack ranged between $4 billion and $8 billion, including ransom payments, recovery efforts, and operational downtime. - *Reputation Damage:* The attack highlighted the vulnerabilities in IT systems and the importance of timely software updates, impacting trust in organizational cybersecurity practices.

Scenario 2: Equifax Data Breach (2017)

In 2017, Equifax, one of the largest credit reporting agencies in the U.S., experienced a massive data breach that exposed the personal information of approximately 147 million Americans. The breach was due to a vulnerability in a web application framework, Apache Struts, which Equifax had failed to patch.

Impact: - *Personal Information Exposure:* The stolen data included Social Security numbers, birth dates, and addresses, making it highly valuable for identity theft and financial fraud. - *Financial Repercussions:* Equifax faced costs exceeding $4 billion, including legal fees, settlements, and remediation efforts. The breach also led to a significant drop in stock value. - *Regulatory and Reputational Damage:* The breach led to increased scrutiny from regulators and damaged Equifax's reputation, affecting customer trust and prompting calls for stronger data protection measures.

Scenario 3: SolarWinds Cyberattack (2020)

In December 2020, the SolarWinds cyberattack, also known as the SolarWinds hack, was discovered. A sophisticated supply chain attack targeted SolarWinds, an IT management company. Attackers inserted malicious code into SolarWinds' Orion software updates, which were then distributed to thousands of customers, including government agencies and major corporations.

Impact: - *Government and Corporate Intrusion:* The attack led to unauthorized access to sensitive data and systems of multiple U.S. government agencies and large corporations, including the Department of Homeland Security and FireEye. - *Long-term Damage:* The extent of the damage was extensive, with long-term implications for national security and corporate data integrity. The breach showcased the vulnerabilities in supply chain security and advanced persistent threats. - *Increased Security Measures:* The attack highlighted the need for enhanced monitoring and security measures across supply chains, leading to increased focus on cybersecurity standards and practices.

These scenarios demonstrate the diverse impacts of cyberbreaches, from operational disruptions and financial losses to long-term damage to reputation and national security.

1.4 Quiz - The Basis of Cybersecurity

1. What does cybersecurity primarily aim to protect?

    ☐ Physical assets
    ☐ Digital information and systems
    ☐ Personal information
    ☐ Intellectual property

2. What is a common method used to secure data transmission over the internet?

    ☐ File Compression
    ☐ Encryption
    ☐ Data Backup
    ☐ Access Control

3. What does a firewall primarily do?

    ☐ Encrypts data
    ☐ Filters and controls incoming and outgoing traffic
    ☐ Monitors network performance
    ☐ Manages user access

4. Which of the following is considered a cybersecurity threat?

    ☐ Software updates
    ☐ Strong passwords
    ☐ Network segmentation
    ☐ Malware

5. What is the purpose of a cybersecurity incident response plan?

    ☐ To respond to and recover from security incidents
    ☐ To increase system speed
    ☐ To manage user access
    ☐ To perform regular backups

6. Which of the following is a type of attack that targets data integrity?

    ☐ Data Tampering
    ☐ Denial of Service (DoS)

☐ Phishing
☐ Man-in-the-Middle

7. What does the acronym VPN stand for?

   ☐ Virtual Private Network
   ☐ Variable Private Network
   ☐ Verified Privacy Network
   ☐ Virtual Public Network

8. What is an example of a physical security measure?

   ☐ Encryption
   ☐ Security tokens
   ☐ Multi-Factor Authentication
   ☐ Biometric access controls

9. What does the acronym SSL stand for?

   ☐ Secure Sockets Layer
   ☐ Secure System Layer
   ☐ System Security Layer
   ☐ Security Sockets Layer

10. Which type of attack involves intercepting communication between two parties?

    ☐ Phishing
    ☐ Man-in-the-Middle
    ☐ DoS Attack
    ☐ SQL Injection

11. What is the primary function of an antivirus software?

    ☐ To detect and remove malicious software
    ☐ To manage user passwords
    ☐ To encrypt data
    ☐ To monitor network performance

12. What does MFA stand for?

    ☐ Multi-Factor Authentication

☐ Multiple-Factor Authentication
☐ Managed-Factor Authentication
☐ Multi-Factor Authentication

13. What is the role of a Security Operations Center (SOC)?

☐ To develop security policies
☐ To perform system backups
☐ To monitor and respond to security threats
☐ To manage user access

14. What does the acronym IDS stand for?

☐ Intrusion Detection System
☐ Intrusion Detection System
☐ Internal Detection System
☐ Internet Detection System

15. Which of the following is a method for protecting data during storage?

☐ Encryption
☐ Firewalls
☐ Access Control
☐ Backup Solutions

16. What is the purpose of a vulnerability assessment?

☐ To identify and evaluate security weaknesses
☐ To improve network speed
☐ To manage user access
☐ To encrypt sensitive data

17. What does the acronym APT stand for?

☐ Advanced Persistent Threat
☐ Automated Prevention Tool
☐ Advanced Persistent Threat
☐ Automated Protection Technique

18. What is a key characteristic of ransomware?

☐ It encrypts files and demands payment for decryption
☐ It monitors network traffic
☐ It manages user permissions
☐ It protects against unauthorized access

19. What is an example of a logical security control?

☐ Password Protection
☐ Physical Locks
☐ Firewalls
☐ Security Cameras

20. What does the acronym DLP stand for?

☐ Data Loss Prevention
☐ Data Leakage Protection
☐ Data Link Protocol
☐ Digital Loss Prevention

21. What is a common example of social engineering?

☐ Phishing
☐ SQL Injection
☐ Phishing
☐ Man-in-the-Middle Attack

22. What is the primary purpose of network segmentation?

☐ To improve network performance
☐ To isolate and protect network segments
☐ To manage user access
☐ To encrypt data

23. What does the acronym HIPAA stand for?

☐ Health Insurance Portability and Accountability Act
☐ Health Information Protection and Accountability Act
☐ Health Insurance Portability and Accountability Act
☐ Health Information Privacy and Access Act

24. Which type of security control involves regular updates and patches?

☐ Physical Control
☐ Administrative Control
☐ Technical Control
☐ Operational Control

25. What is a common use of a public key infrastructure (PKI)?

☐ To manage user permissions
☐ To provide secure communications using digital certificates
☐ To monitor network traffic
☐ To encrypt stored data

26. What is the primary purpose of access control lists (ACLs)?

☐ To define permissions for accessing resources
☐ To encrypt network traffic
☐ To manage user accounts
☐ To monitor network performance

27. What is a common feature of two-factor authentication (2FA)?

☐ Requires two different types of authentication factors
☐ Uses a single password for access
☐ Encrypts data during transmission
☐ Requires both something you know and something you have

28. What does the acronym IoT stand for?

☐ Internet of Things
☐ Internet of Things
☐ Internal Operational Technology
☐ Integrated Online Technology

29. What is the purpose of a patch management process?

☐ To monitor network traffic
☐ To apply updates and fix vulnerabilities
☐ To manage user access
☐ To perform regular backups

30. What does the acronym MFA stand for?

☐ Multi-Factor Authentication
☐ Multiple-Factor Authentication
☐ Managed-Factor Authentication
☐ Multi-Factor Authorization

31. What type of attack involves overwhelming a system with traffic?

☐ SQL Injection
☐ Denial of Service (DoS)
☐ Phishing
☐ Cross-Site Scripting (XSS)

32. What is the primary function of a Security Information and Event Management (SIEM) system?

☐ To manage user accounts
☐ To collect and analyze security event data
☐ To perform system backups
☐ To encrypt data

33. What does the acronym RTO stand for in disaster recovery planning?

☐ Recovery Time Objective
☐ Recovery Time Operation
☐ Restoration Time Objective
☐ Response Time Objective

34. What is a common method for ensuring data availability?

☐ Data Encryption
☐ Regular Backups
☐ Access Control
☐ Network Segmentation

35. What is the main goal of risk management in cybersecurity?

☐ To prevent all possible threats
☐ To identify, assess, and mitigate risks
☐ To monitor system performance
☐ To manage user access

36. What does the acronym GDPR stand for?

    ☐ General Data Protection Regulation
    ☐ General Digital Privacy Regulation
    ☐ Government Data Protection Regulation
    ☐ Global Data Privacy Regulation

37. What is a common feature of an intrusion detection system (IDS)?

    ☐ Prevents unauthorized access
    ☐ Monitors and analyzes network traffic for suspicious activity
    ☐ Encrypts data during transmission
    ☐ Manages user accounts

38. What is an example of a cybersecurity best practice?

    ☐ Using weak passwords
    ☐ Regularly updating software
    ☐ Disabling firewalls
    ☐ Ignoring security alerts

39. What does the acronym PCI DSS stand for?

    ☐ Payment Card Industry Data Security Standard
    ☐ Payment Card Information Data Security Standard
    ☐ Public Card Industry Data Security Standard
    ☐ Payment Card Internal Data Security Standard

40. What is the purpose of a security policy?

    ☐ To define rules and guidelines for securing information
    ☐ To manage user permissions
    ☐ To monitor network traffic
    ☐ To perform regular backups

41. What does the acronym SSH stand for?

    ☐ Secure Shell
    ☐ Secure Socket Handling
    ☐ System Security Hub
    ☐ Secure Server Host

42. What is a primary goal of data protection laws?

☐ To increase network speed
☐ To manage system performance
☐ To protect individuals' personal data from unauthorized access
☐ To encrypt internal communications

43. What does the acronym RTO stand for in business continuity?

☐ Recovery Time Objective
☐ Recovery Time Operation
☐ Restoration Time Objective
☐ Response Time Optimization

44. What is a primary function of intrusion prevention systems (IPS)?

☐ To detect and block potential threats
☐ To monitor network traffic
☐ To encrypt data
☐ To manage user accounts

45. What does the acronym AUP stand for in cybersecurity?

☐ Acceptable Use Policy
☐ Automated Use Protocol
☐ Advanced User Protection
☐ Access User Policy

46. What is a common feature of multi-factor authentication (MFA)?

☐ Requires only a password
☐ Uses a single authentication method
☐ Requires multiple forms of identification
☐ Relies solely on biometric data

47. What does the acronym NAC stand for in network security?

☐ Network Access Control
☐ Network Authentication Center
☐ Network Application Control
☐ Network Access Check

48. What is an example of a logical access control?

☐ Physical security badges
☐ Locked server rooms
☐ Passwords
☐ Security cameras

49. What does the acronym EDR stand for in cybersecurity?

☐ Endpoint Detection and Response
☐ External Data Recovery
☐ Endpoint Detection and Response
☐ Enhanced Data Reporting

50. What is a common cybersecurity strategy to prevent unauthorized access?

☐ Implementing strong passwords and multi-factor authentication
☐ Regularly updating software
☐ Monitoring network traffic
☐ Performing system backups

51. What does the acronym VPN stand for?

☐ Virtual Private Network
☐ Variable Private Network
☐ Verified Privacy Network
☐ Virtual Public Network

52. What is the purpose of data masking?

☐ To hide sensitive data while maintaining its usability
☐ To encrypt data during transmission
☐ To create data backups
☐ To manage user permissions

53. What does the acronym SOC stand for in cybersecurity?

☐ Security Operations Center
☐ Security Online Control
☐ System Operations Center

☐ Secure Operations Center

54. What is an example of a network security protocol?

   ☐ SSH
   ☐ HTTPS
   ☐ FTP
   ☐ Telnet

55. What is the primary purpose of a security audit?

   ☐ To perform system backups
   ☐ To evaluate and improve security measures
   ☐ To manage user access
   ☐ To monitor network traffic

56. What does the acronym SIEM stand for?

   ☐ Security Information and Event Management
   ☐ Security Integrated Event Management
   ☐ System Information and Event Management
   ☐ Security Incident and Event Monitoring

57. What is a common type of security vulnerability in web applications?

   ☐ SQL Injection
   ☐ Cross-Site Scripting (XSS)
   ☐ Denial of Service (DoS)
   ☐ Phishing

58. What is the role of a penetration test?

   ☐ To manage user access
   ☐ To identify and exploit vulnerabilities in a system
   ☐ To perform data encryption
   ☐ To monitor network traffic

59. What does the acronym NIST stand for in cybersecurity frameworks?

   ☐ National Institute of Standards and Technology

☐ National Information Security Trust
☐ National Institute for Security Technology
☐ National Information Standards and Technology

60. What is the purpose of data encryption?

☐ To protect data from unauthorized access
☐ To manage network traffic
☐ To create data backups
☐ To monitor system performance

61. What does the acronym TLP stand for in information sharing?

☐ Traffic Light Protocol
☐ Technical Level Protocol
☐ Tactical Level Protocol
☐ Transfer Level Protocol

62. What is a primary goal of a business continuity plan?

☐ To ensure operations can continue during and after a disruption
☐ To manage user access
☐ To encrypt data
☐ To monitor network performance

63. What does the acronym IDS stand for in network security?

☐ Intrusion Detection System
☐ Internal Detection System
☐ Internet Detection System
☐ Integrated Detection System

64. What is an example of a data breach notification requirement?

☐ Notify affected individuals within a specific timeframe
☐ Inform relevant authorities and affected parties
☐ Increase network bandwidth
☐ Encrypt all affected data

65. What is the primary goal of an incident response team?

☐ To manage and mitigate security incidents
☐ To perform regular backups
☐ To monitor network traffic
☐ To manage user access

66. What does the acronym CIA stand for in cybersecurity principles?

☐ Confidentiality, Integrity, Availability
☐ Confidentiality, Identity, Access
☐ Control, Integrity, Access
☐ Confidentiality, Identification, Authorization

67. What is a key benefit of using strong, unique passwords?

☐ To reduce the risk of unauthorized access
☐ To improve system performance
☐ To monitor network traffic
☐ To manage user permissions

68. What does the acronym SOC stand for in cybersecurity?

☐ Security Operations Center
☐ Security Online Control
☐ System Operations Center
☐ Secure Operations Center

69. What is the role of encryption in data security?

☐ To protect data by making it unreadable to unauthorized users
☐ To monitor network performance
☐ To manage user access
☐ To perform regular backups

70. What is a common cybersecurity measure for protecting endpoints?

☐ Network Segmentation
☐ Endpoint Protection Software
☐ Data Encryption
☐ Firewall Configuration

71. What does the acronym CSIRT stand for?

☐ Computer Security Incident Response Team
☐ Computer Security Integration Response Team
☐ Cyber Security Incident Response Team
☐ Computer System Incident Response Team

72. What is a common tool used for vulnerability scanning?

☐ Firewall
☐ Vulnerability Scanner
☐ Intrusion Detection System
☐ Encryption Software

73. What is the primary purpose of data classification?

☐ To categorize data based on its sensitivity and value
☐ To perform data encryption
☐ To monitor network traffic
☐ To manage user access

74. What does the acronym RPO stand for in disaster recovery planning?

☐ Recovery Point Objective
☐ Recovery Performance Objective
☐ Restoration Point Objective
☐ Response Point Objective

75. What is a common method for securing a wireless network?

☐ Using strong encryption (e.g., WPA3)
☐ Regularly updating firmware
☐ Monitoring network traffic
☐ Implementing network segmentation

76. What does the acronym BYOD stand for?

☐ Bring Your Own Device
☐ Bring Your Own Data
☐ Bring Your Own Disk
☐ Bring Your Own Domain

1.5 Answers to The Questions

Great! Now, to check your answers:

1. Digital information and systems Physical assets

2. Encryption

3. Filters and controls incoming and outgoing traffic

4. Malware

5. To respond to and recover from security incidents

6. Data Tampering

7. Virtual Private Network

8. Biometric access controls

9. Secure Sockets Layer

10. Man-in-the-Middle

11. To detect and remove malicious software

12. Multi-Factor Authentication

13. To monitor and respond to security threats

14. Intrusion Detection System

15. Encryption

16. To identify and evaluate security weaknesses

17. Advanced Persistent Threat

18. It encrypts files and demands payment for decryption

19. Firewalls

20. Data Loss Prevention

21. Phishing

22. To isolate and protect network segments

23. Health Insurance Portability and Accountability Act

24. Technical Control

25. To provide secure communications using digital certificates

26. To define permissions for accessing resources

27. Requires both something you know and something you have

28. Internet of Things

29. To apply updates and fix vulnerabilities

30. Multi-Factor Authentication

31. Denial of Service (DoS)

32. To collect and analyze security event data

33. Recovery Time Objective

34. Regular Backups

35. To identify, assess, and mitigate risks

36. General Data Protection Regulation

37. Monitors and analyzes network traffic for suspicious activity

38. Regularly updating software

39. Payment Card Industry Data Security Standard

40. To define rules and guidelines for securing information

41. Secure Shell

42. To protect individuals' personal data from unauthorized access

43. Recovery Time Objective

44. To detect and block potential threats

45. Acceptable Use Policy

46. Requires multiple forms of identification

47. Network Access Control

48. Passwords

49. Endpoint Detection and Response

50. Implementing strong passwords and multi-factor authentication

51. Virtual Private Network

52. To hide sensitive data while maintaining its usability

53. Security Operations Center

54. HTTPS

55. To evaluate and improve security measures

56. Security Information and Event Management

57. Cross-Site Scripting (XSS)

58. To identify and exploit vulnerabilities in a system

59. National Institute of Standards and Technology

60. To protect data from unauthorized access

61. Traffic Light Protocol

62. To ensure operations can continue during and after a disruption

63. Intrusion Detection System

64. Inform relevant authorities and affected parties

65. To manage and mitigate security incidents

66. Confidentiality, Integrity, Availability

67. To reduce the risk of unauthorized access

68. Security Operations Center

69. To protect data by making it unreadable to unauthorized users

70. Endpoint Protection Software

71. Computer Security Incident Response Team

72. Vulnerability Scanner

73. To categorize data based on its sensitivity and value

74. Recovery Point Objective

75. Using strong encryption (e.g., WPA3)

76. Bring Your Own Device

Chapter 2: Fundamentals of Network Architecture

2.1   Mastering Network Basics

Mastering network basics involves understanding the fundamental types of networks, topologies, protocols, and devices that form the backbone of modern IT infrastructure. Networks can be categorized into several types based on their geographical scope and purpose. Local Area Networks (LANs) connect devices within a confined area such as an office or campus, allowing for high-speed communication and resource sharing. Wide Area Networks (WANs) span larger geographical areas, connecting multiple LANs across cities or even continents. Metropolitan Area Networks (MANs) bridge the gap between LANs and WANs, serving larger areas like cities, while Personal Area Networks (PANs) connect devices over very short distances, such as between a smartphone and a Bluetooth headset.

Understanding network topologies is crucial for designing efficient and reliable networks. Common topologies include bus, star, ring, mesh, and hybrid configurations. A bus topology uses a single central cable to connect all devices, which can lead to performance issues if the central bus fails. A star topology connects devices to a central hub, offering better performance and easier troubleshooting but relying on the central hub's reliability. Ring topologies connect devices in a circular fashion, which can be efficient but problematic if any device fails. Mesh topologies provide multiple redundant paths between devices, enhancing reliability but increasing complexity. Hybrid topologies combine elements of different topologies to meet specific needs and requirements.

Networking protocols define the rules for data exchange between devices, ensuring smooth and reliable communication. Key protocols include Transmission Control Protocol (TCP), which ensures the reliable transmission of data by establishing connections and managing packet order. Internet Protocol (IP) addresses and routes packets across networks, with IPv4 and IPv6 providing address schemes for various network sizes. Hypertext Transfer Protocol (HTTP) is fundamental for web communication, enabling the transfer of web pages. File Transfer Protocol (FTP) facilitates file transfers between clients and servers, while Simple Mail Transfer Protocol (SMTP) handles email routing. Mastery of these protocols and understanding networking devices like routers, switches, and access points are essential for building, managing, and securing effective network infrastructures.

2.2   Networks of Devices

In the realm of networking, the term "networks of devices" refers to interconnected systems that allow multiple devices to communicate, share resources, and collaborate. At the core of such networks are various devices, each serving specific roles to facilitate seamless communication and data exchange. Common devices in a network include computers, printers, servers, routers, switches, and access points. These devices are interconnected through physical cables or wireless connections, forming the infrastructure that enables networks to function effectively. Understanding how these devices interact is crucial for managing and optimizing network performance.

A network's efficiency is heavily influenced by the types of connections and the topology used. Devices can be connected using wired technologies, such as Ethernet cables, which provide stable and high-speed connections, or wireless technologies like Wi-Fi, which offer flexibility and mobility. The choice between wired and wireless connections impacts the network's speed, reliability, and coverage. In a typical network setup, routers and switches play central roles; routers connect different networks and manage data traffic, while switches facilitate communication within a local network by directing data to the appropriate devices based on their addresses. Access points extend the reach of wireless networks, enabling devices to connect from a broader area.

Network design also considers scalability and security to ensure robust and adaptable systems. As networks grow, additional devices and connections need to be integrated without compromising performance. Effective network management involves monitoring traffic, managing bandwidth, and ensuring secure access to prevent unauthorized usage.

Security measures, such as firewalls and encryption, protect the network from potential threats and vulnerabilities. Understanding the interplay between different devices and network components helps in designing efficient, secure, and scalable networks that meet the needs of organizations and users alike.

2.3   How to Correctly Design a Network

Designing a network correctly is a critical task that requires careful planning and consideration of various factors to ensure it meets organizational needs and can scale effectively. The first step in network design is to conduct a thorough needs assessment. This involves understanding the specific requirements of the organization, including the number of users, types of applications, and data traffic patterns. By identifying these needs, you can determine the appropriate network size, capacity, and performance criteria. This phase also includes evaluating the current infrastructure, if any, to integrate new components smoothly and avoid redundancy.

Once the needs assessment is complete, the next step is to choose an appropriate network topology and architecture. The network topology defines the layout of network devices and connections, influencing factors such as performance, scalability, and reliability. Common topologies include star, ring, mesh, and hybrid configurations. For instance, a star topology, with devices connected to a central switch or hub, is often used in office environments for its ease of management and fault tolerance. Additionally, network architects must consider whether to use wired, wireless, or a combination of both technologies, based on factors like coverage area, speed requirements, and budget constraints. The design should also include considerations for redundancy and failover mechanisms to ensure network availability in case of hardware failures.

Finally, implementing robust security measures and ensuring effective network management are crucial for maintaining a secure and efficient network. Security design involves configuring firewalls, intrusion detection systems, and encryption protocols to protect against unauthorized access and cyber threats. Network management includes setting up monitoring tools to track performance, manage bandwidth, and troubleshoot issues proactively. Additionally, designing for scalability involves planning for future growth by allowing easy expansion of network resources and incorporating flexible configurations.

Proper documentation of the network design, including diagrams and configuration details, is essential for maintenance and troubleshooting, ensuring that the network remains resilient and adaptable to changing needs.

2.4   Network Topologies and Configurations

Network topologies and configurations are fundamental aspects of network design that determine how devices are arranged and how data flows through a network. **Topology** refers to the physical or logical layout of network devices and their connections. Common network topologies include **star**, **bus**, **ring**, **mesh**, and **hybrid** configurations. Each topology has unique characteristics that influence network performance, reliability, and scalability. For instance, a **star topology** connects all devices to a central hub or switch, offering simplicity and ease of management but creating a single point of failure. In contrast, a **mesh topology** connects each device to several others, providing high redundancy and reliability but at a higher cost and complexity.

The choice of network configuration affects how data is transmitted and how efficiently the network operates. In a **star topology**, all network traffic is routed through the central hub or switch, which can lead to better performance and ease of troubleshooting, but any failure in the central device can disrupt the entire network. A **bus topology**, where all devices share a single central cable, is cost-effective and easy to set up but can suffer from data collisions and performance issues as the network grows. A **ring topology** connects devices in a circular fashion, where each device acts as a repeater to the next, providing orderly data transmission but potential delays and issues if any device fails.

Hybrid topologies combine elements of different topologies to leverage their respective advantages while mitigating their drawbacks. For example, a **star-bus topology** combines the scalability of a bus topology with the central management of a star topology. Configurations should also consider the **network size**, **traffic patterns**, and **expansion plans**. Effective network design involves selecting a topology that aligns with the organization's needs, ensuring optimal performance, ease of management, and scalability. Network configurations must be tailored to specific requirements, incorporating redundancy and failover mechanisms to enhance reliability and minimize downtime.

2.5   Secure Corporate Networks

Securing corporate networks is crucial to protecting sensitive data and maintaining the integrity of organizational operations. The first step in securing a corporate network is to implement a robust network architecture that includes multiple layers of security. This typically involves deploying firewalls, which act as barriers between internal networks and external threats by filtering incoming and outgoing traffic. Intrusion Detection Systems (IDS) and Intrusion Prevention Systems (IPS) are also essential, as they monitor network traffic for signs of suspicious activity and take proactive measures to prevent potential breaches. Additionally, segmenting the network into different zones or subnets can help contain any security incidents and limit the spread of malware.

Another key aspect of securing corporate networks is ensuring that all devices and applications are up-to-date with the latest security patches and updates. Vulnerabilities in software and hardware can be exploited by attackers, so regular patch management is critical. Implementing strong access controls is also vital; this includes enforcing the principle of least privilege, which restricts user access to only the resources necessary for their roles. Multi-factor authentication (MFA) further enhances security by requiring additional verification beyond just a password. Regularly reviewing and updating access permissions and authentication methods helps prevent unauthorized access and potential insider threats.

Finally, educating employees and conducting regular security awareness training is fundamental to maintaining a secure corporate network. Employees are often the first line of defense against cyber threats, and their understanding of security best practices can significantly reduce the risk of accidental breaches or phishing attacks. Security policies and procedures should be clearly communicated, and employees should be trained on recognizing and responding to potential security threats. Additionally, conducting regular security audits and penetration testing helps identify vulnerabilities and weaknesses in the network, allowing organizations to address them proactively. By combining strong technical defenses with a well-informed workforce, corporations can better protect their networks from evolving cyber threats.

2.6 Quiz: Understanding Networks

1. What does **network topology** refer to?

   ☐ The physical or logical layout of network devices and connections
   ☐ The speed of the network connection
   ☐ The amount of data transferred per second
   ☐ The methods used for data encryption

2. In a **star topology**, how are devices connected?

   ☐ Each device connects to multiple other devices directly
   ☐ All devices connect to a central hub or switch
   ☐ Devices are arranged in a circular fashion
   ☐ Devices are connected in a single line

3. Which topology connects devices in a circular fashion?

   ☐ Star
   ☐ Ring
   ☐ Bus
   ☐ Mesh

4. What is the main advantage of a **mesh topology**?

   ☐ Simplicity in design
   ☐ Lower cost
   ☐ High redundancy and reliability
   ☐ Ease of troubleshooting

5. Which network device connects different networks and manages data traffic?

   ☐ Switch
   ☐ Router
   ☐ Hub
   ☐ Access Point

6. What does a **bus topology** use to connect devices?

   ☐ A central hub

☐ A circular connection
☐ A single central cable
☐ Multiple redundant paths

7. In a **star topology**, what is a potential drawback?

☐ High cost
☐ Single point of failure
☐ Complexity
☐ Lack of redundancy

8. Which device facilitates communication within a local network by directing data?

☐ Router
☐ Access Point
☐ Switch
☐ Hub

9. What is the main advantage of a **hybrid topology**?

☐ Lower cost
☐ Simplicity
☐ Combination of different topologies' advantages
☐ Standardization

10. Which topology is known for its cost-effectiveness and ease of setup?

☐ Star
☐ Mesh
☐ Bus
☐ Ring

11. What is the primary role of a **firewall** in a network?

☐ To connect different networks
☐ To monitor network traffic
☐ To filter and block unauthorized access
☐ To manage internal data routing

12. Which network topology is best for handling high traffic loads

without a single point of failure?

- ☐ Star
- ☐ Bus
- ☐ Ring
- ☐ Mesh

13. What does the term **network segmentation** refer to?

- ☐ Connecting all devices to a central hub
- ☐ Dividing a network into smaller sub-networks
- ☐ Using multiple cables for connections
- ☐ Integrating wireless and wired technologies

14. What is the purpose of **intrusion detection systems** (IDS)?

- ☐ To connect different networks
- ☐ To manage network traffic
- ☐ To monitor and detect suspicious activities
- ☐ To provide network redundancy

15. Which device extends the reach of a wireless network?

- ☐ Router
- ☐ Switch
- ☐ Access Point
- ☐ Hub

16. In a **ring topology**, what happens if one device fails?

- ☐ The entire network is unaffected
- ☐ The network may experience delays or disruption
- ☐ All devices reconnect automatically
- ☐ Data traffic is rerouted through the central hub

17. What is a key advantage of a **star-bus topology**?

- ☐ Reduced complexity
- ☐ Higher cost
- ☐ Combination of star and bus advantages
- ☐ Limited scalability

18. Which technology is used for connecting devices over very short distances?

    ☐ Wi-Fi
    ☐ Bluetooth
    ☐ Ethernet
    ☐ Cellular

19. What is the main role of a **router** in a network?

    ☐ To connect devices within a local network
    ☐ To extend wireless coverage
    ☐ To connect different networks and manage traffic
    ☐ To filter incoming and outgoing traffic

20. Which topology would be least impacted by a single point of failure?

    ☐ Bus
    ☐ Star
    ☐ Ring
    ☐ Mesh

21. What is the purpose of **patch management** in network security?

    ☐ To monitor network traffic
    ☐ To control user access
    ☐ To apply updates and fix vulnerabilities
    ☐ To configure network devices

22. Which network topology is characterized by its use of a central cable to connect all devices?

    ☐ Star
    ☐ Bus
    ☐ Ring
    ☐ Mesh

23. How does a **switch** differ from a **hub**?

    ☐ A switch broadcasts data to all devices, while a hub directs it to specific devices

☐ A switch directs data to specific devices, while a hub broadcasts it to all devices
☐ A switch is used for wireless connections, while a hub is for wired connections
☐ A switch connects devices across networks, while a hub connects devices within a network

24. Which network device is essential for managing data traffic within a LAN?

☐ Router
☐ Access Point
☐ Switch
☐ Modem

25. In which scenario would a **ring topology** be most appropriate?

☐ Large office networks with high redundancy needs
☐ Small to medium-sized networks with manageable traffic
☐ Networks requiring central management
☐ Environments with high costs and complex setups

26. What is one of the main challenges of a **bus topology**?

☐ High cost and complexity
☐ Poor scalability
☐ Data collisions and performance issues
☐ Limited redundancy

27. How does **network segmentation** enhance security?

☐ By connecting all devices directly
☐ By using a single large subnet
☐ By isolating different network segments to limit the spread of threats
☐ By reducing the number of network devices

28. What is a primary benefit of a **star topology**?

☐ Lower cost and simplicity
☐ Better performance with large numbers of devices
☐ Redundancy in case of device failure

☐ Ease of management and troubleshooting

29. Which of the following is a characteristic of a **mesh topology**?

   ☐ Single point of failure
   ☐ Lower reliability
   ☐ High redundancy and fault tolerance
   ☐ Cost-effectiveness

30. What role does an **access point** play in a wireless network?

   ☐ To connect wired devices to the network
   ☐ To extend wireless network coverage
   ☐ To manage network traffic
   ☐ To filter network traffic

31. What is the purpose of a **hub** in a network?

   ☐ To manage network traffic
   ☐ To connect multiple devices in a network and broadcast data
   ☐ To extend network coverage
   ☐ To filter unauthorized access

32. What does **intrusion prevention** involve?

   ☐ Monitoring network traffic
   ☐ Blocking and responding to potential threats in real-time
   ☐ Managing user access controls
   ☐ Applying software patches

33. Which topology is typically used to reduce network collisions and improve performance?

   ☐ Bus
   ☐ Ring
   ☐ Star
   ☐ Mesh

34. What is the main disadvantage of a **star topology**?

   ☐ High cost and complexity
   ☐ Data collisions

☐ Central hub failure impacts the entire network
☐ Limited scalability

35. In a network, what does a **firewall** primarily protect against?

    ☐ Unauthorized access and cyber threats
    ☐ Hardware malfunctions
    ☐ Data corruption
    ☐ Network performance issues

36. What type of network topology is characterized by high fault tolerance due to its interconnected devices?

    ☐ Star
    ☐ Bus
    ☐ Mesh
    ☐ Ring

37. Which device is used to connect a network to the Internet?

    ☐ Switch
    ☐ Router
    ☐ Hub
    ☐ Access Point

38. What does **network redundancy** refer to?

    ☐ Using a single network path
    ☐ Implementing multiple backup paths or systems
    ☐ Increasing network speed
    ☐ Simplifying network design

39. Which network device helps in isolating network traffic to improve security?

    ☐ Hub
    ☐ Access Point
    ☐ Switch
    ☐ Firewall

40. What is the main purpose of a **VPN** in a network?

- ☐ To connect multiple networks directly
- ☐ To manage internal data traffic
- ☐ To create a secure, encrypted connection over the internet
- ☐ To monitor network performance

41. Which network device acts as a central point for connecting multiple devices in a star topology?

- ☐ Router
- ☐ Access Point
- ☐ Switch
- ☐ Hub

42. What is the primary benefit of implementing a **hybrid topology**?

- ☐ Lower cost
- ☐ Simplicity
- ☐ Combining benefits of different topologies
- ☐ Reduced redundancy

43. Which network topology is least likely to experience performance degradation as more devices are added?

- ☐ Bus
- ☐ Ring
- ☐ Mesh
- ☐ Star

44. What is the primary advantage of using **multi-factor authentication** (MFA)?

- ☐ Simplicity of implementation
- ☐ Lower cost
- ☐ Increased security by requiring multiple forms of verification
- ☐ Faster access to network resources

45. In a **star topology**, what happens if the central hub fails?

- ☐ The entire network is disrupted
- ☐ Only one device is affected
- ☐ The network continues to operate normally
- ☐ Devices automatically reconnect through another hub

46. What does the term **bandwidth** refer to in a network?

☐ The number of devices connected to the network
☐ The physical layout of network connections
☐ The amount of data transferred per second
☐ The type of network topology used

47. What is the primary function of an **intrusion prevention system** (IPS)?

☐ To connect multiple networks
☐ To monitor and log network activity
☐ To block and respond to identified threats in real-time
☐ To provide network management

48. Which topology is generally used in small networks where simplicity is a key factor?

☐ Star
☐ Mesh
☐ Bus
☐ Ring

49. What does **QoS** stand for in network management?

☐ Quality of Service
☐ Quality of Service
☐ Quick Operating System
☐ Quantitative Online Security

50. Which network device is used primarily for filtering traffic and protecting the network perimeter?

☐ Router
☐ Switch
☐ Hub
☐ Firewall

51. What is the main advantage of a **star topology** over a **bus topology**?

☐ Lower cost
☐ Simplicity

☐ Better fault tolerance and easier troubleshooting
☐ Reduced number of connections

52. How does a **hub** differ from a **switch** in terms of data handling?

☐ A hub sends data only to its intended recipient
☐ A switch broadcasts data to all connected devices
☐ A hub broadcasts data to all connected devices, while a switch sends data only to the intended recipient
☐ A switch connects devices to the Internet, while a hub connects them to the LAN

53. What is the purpose of **network addressing**?

☐ To encrypt data transmitted over the network
☐ To assign unique identifiers to devices for communication
☐ To manage network traffic
☐ To connect different network segments

54. Which of the following is a common type of network attack?

☐ Network segmentation
☐ Denial of Service (DoS)
☐ Load balancing
☐ Data encryption

55. What is a **virtual private network** (VPN) used for?

☐ To increase network speed
☐ To connect devices in a local network
☐ To secure communications over a public network
☐ To manage network devices

56. What does **bandwidth** determine in a network?

☐ The type of network cables used
☐ The number of connected devices
☐ The maximum rate of data transfer
☐ The physical layout of the network

57. What is one of the main benefits of using a **firewall**?

☐ To manage data storage
☐ To provide internet connectivity
☐ To connect devices within a network
☐ To filter and block unauthorized access

58. Which network topology involves each device connecting to multiple other devices?

☐ Star
☐ Mesh
☐ Bus
☐ Ring

59. What is the primary advantage of a **bus topology**?

☐ High redundancy
☐ Easy expansion
☐ High cost
☐ Simple setup and low cost

60. What is the function of **network segmentation** in improving network performance?

☐ By connecting all devices to a central hub
☐ By reducing traffic congestion in each segment
☐ By simplifying network design
☐ By increasing the number of devices

61. How does a **hybrid topology** enhance a network's capabilities?

☐ By using a single topology type
☐ By combining the benefits of different topology types
☐ By simplifying network design
☐ By reducing network cost

62. What does **QoS** stand for, and why is it important?

☐ Quality of Service; it ensures prioritization of critical network traffic
☐ Quality of Software; it improves software performance
☐ Quantity of Security; it measures security levels
☐ Quick Operating System; it speeds up system performance

63. Which network device is commonly used to extend a wired network over a larger area?

   ☐ Router
   ☐ Hub
   ☐ Switch
   ☐ Access Point

64. What is the primary role of a **hub** in a network?

   ☐ To manage and route network traffic
   ☐ To provide network security
   ☐ To connect multiple devices and broadcast data
   ☐ To extend network coverage

65. What does a **switch** do to improve network efficiency?

   ☐ Broadcasts data to all connected devices
   ☐ Connects devices to the Internet
   ☐ Sends data only to the intended recipient
   ☐ Provides network redundancy

66. What is one advantage of using a **ring topology**?

   ☐ Simple setup
   ☐ Data packets travel in a predictable path
   ☐ High fault tolerance
   ☐ High cost

67. In which situation is a **star topology** most beneficial?

   ☐ In small, simple networks
   ☐ When cost is a major concern
   ☐ In networks requiring easy management and troubleshooting
   ☐ For very high-speed data transfer

68. What does **network management** typically involve?

   ☐ Only hardware setup
   ☐ Only software installation
   ☐ Monitoring, maintaining, and optimizing network performance

☐ Only security measures

69. What is the benefit of using a **router** in a network?

    ☐ To extend wireless coverage
    ☐ To manage internal data routing
    ☐ To connect different networks and manage traffic
    ☐ To filter network traffic

70. Which network device is designed to direct data to specific devices within a network?

    ☐ Hub
    ☐ Router
    ☐ Switch
    ☐ Access Point

71. What is a major advantage of **network segmentation**?

    ☐ Connecting all devices with one cable
    ☐ Simplifying the network design
    ☐ Reducing the overall cost
    ☐ Enhancing security and reducing congestion

72. What is the primary function of a **firewall**?

    ☐ To manage network performance
    ☐ To protect the network by filtering unauthorized access
    ☐ To extend network range
    ☐ To connect devices

73. What type of topology is known for having the most redundancy?

    ☐ Star
    ☐ Bus
    ☐ Mesh
    ☐ Ring

74. How does a **mesh topology** support fault tolerance?

    ☐ By having a single point of failure
    ☐ By reducing the number of connections

☐ By allowing multiple paths for data to travel
☐ By centralizing network management

75. What is the primary goal of **intrusion detection**?

☐ To block threats in real-time
☐ To monitor and identify potential security breaches
☐ To manage user access
☐ To secure network devices

76. Which network topology is generally most cost-effective?

☐ Bus
☐ Star
☐ Mesh
☐ Ring

77. What does a **virtual private network** (VPN) provide?

☐ Increased network speed
☐ Enhanced network hardware
☐ Secure remote access over the internet
☐ Simplified network management

78. What is one key characteristic of a **hub**?

☐ It filters network traffic
☐ It routes data to specific devices
☐ It broadcasts data to all connected devices
☐ It provides network security

79. What is the main advantage of using a **switch** over a **hub**?

☐ Lower cost
☐ Simpler setup
☐ More efficient data handling by sending data only to the intended recipient
☐ Greater redundancy

80. What does **network performance** encompass?

☐ Only the speed of data transfer

☐ Only the reliability of the network
☐ Both speed and reliability of the network
☐ Only the number of connected devices

81. Which topology is known for its straightforward implementation and maintenance?

☐ Star
☐ Mesh
☐ Bus
☐ Ring

82. What does **network security** involve?

☐ Only software protection
☐ Only hardware protection
☐ Protecting both hardware and software from unauthorized access and attacks
☐ Only network performance monitoring

83. Which of the following is a typical use for a **router**?

☐ To extend network coverage
☐ To connect different networks and manage traffic
☐ To provide wireless access
☐ To filter network traffic

84. What does **network bandwidth** measure?

☐ The number of network devices
☐ The physical network layout
☐ The maximum data transfer rate of the network
☐ The type of network topology

85. What is one main feature of a **ring topology**?

☐ Centralized management
☐ Data travels in one direction or both directions in a loop
☐ High cost
☐ High fault tolerance

86. How does **network segmentation** help in troubleshooting network

issues?

- [ ] By connecting all devices to a single network segment
- [ ] By isolating problems within specific segments
- [ ] By simplifying the network topology
- [ ] By reducing the number of network devices

87. What is a **VPN** used for in network security?

- [ ] To create a physical network connection
- [ ] To provide secure and encrypted communication over a public network
- [ ] To extend network coverage
- [ ] To monitor network performance

88. What is the main advantage of **network redundancy**?

- [ ] Lower cost
- [ ] Simplicity
- [ ] Increased reliability and fault tolerance
- [ ] Reduced network speed

89. What does **quality of service (QoS)** ensure in a network?

- [ ] Lower cost of network hardware
- [ ] Prioritization of critical network traffic
- [ ] Increased bandwidth
- [ ] Simplified network design

90. What role does a **firewall** play in network security?

- [ ] It monitors network performance
- [ ] It extends the network range
- [ ] It filters and blocks unauthorized access
- [ ] It connects devices within the network

91. How does a **mesh topology** differ from a **star topology**?

- [ ] A mesh topology is simpler to implement than a star topology
- [ ] A star topology has higher redundancy than a mesh topology
- [ ] A mesh topology offers higher redundancy due to multiple connections between devices

☐ A mesh topology has a central hub, while a star topology does not

92. What does **network performance** typically include?

☐ Only network security
☐ Only network topology
☐ Both speed and reliability of the network
☐ Only the number of devices

93. Which network device is primarily used to connect multiple devices within a single network segment?

☐ Router
☐ Switch
☐ Hub
☐ Access Point

94. What is the main advantage of a **bus topology** over other topologies?

☐ High fault tolerance
☐ High cost
☐ Easy scalability
☐ Simplicity and low cost

95. How does **network redundancy** improve reliability?

☐ By reducing the number of connections
☐ By centralizing network management
☐ By providing multiple paths for data to travel
☐ By simplifying network design

96. What is the function of a **hub** in a network?

☐ To connect devices and filter data
☐ To provide network security
☐ To manage network traffic
☐ To connect multiple devices and broadcast data to all

2.7 Answers to The Questions

Great! Now, check your answers:

1. The methods used for data encryption

2. All devices connect to a central hub or switch

3. Ring

4. High redundancy and reliability

5. Router

6. A single central cable

7. Single point of failure

8. Switch

9. Combination of different topologies' advantages

10. Bus

11. To filter and block unauthorized access

12. Mesh

13. Dividing a network into smaller sub-networks

14. To monitor and detect suspicious activities

15. Access Point

16. The network may experience delays or disruption

17. Combination of star and bus advantages

18. Bluetooth

19. To connect different networks and manage traffic

20. Mesh

21. To apply updates and fix vulnerabilities

22. Bus

23. A switch directs data to specific devices, while a hub broadcasts it to all devices

24. Switch

25. Small to medium-sized networks with manageable traffic

26. Data collisions and performance issues

27. By isolating different network segments to limit the spread of threats

28. Ease of management and troubleshooting

29. High redundancy and fault tolerance

30. To extend wireless network coverage

31. To connect multiple devices in a network and broadcast data

32. Blocking and responding to potential threats in real-time

33. Star

34. Central hub failure impacts the entire network

35. Unauthorized access and cyber threats

36. Mesh

37. Router

38. Implementing multiple backup paths or systems

39. Firewall

40. To create a secure, encrypted connection over the internet

41. Switch

42. Combining benefits of different topologies

43. Mesh

44. Increased security by requiring multiple forms of verification

45. The entire network is disrupted

46. The amount of data transferred per second

47. To block and respond to identified threats in real-time

48. Bus

49. Quality of Service

50. Firewall

51. Better fault tolerance and easier troubleshooting

52. A hub broadcasts data to all connected devices, while a switch sends data only to the intended recipient

53. To assign unique identifiers to devices for communication

54. Denial of Service (DoS)

55. To secure communications over a public network

56. The maximum rate of data transfer

57. To filter and block unauthorized access

58. Mesh

59. Simple setup and low cost

60. By reducing traffic congestion in each segment

61. By combining the benefits of different topology types

62. Quality of Service; it ensures prioritization of critical network traffic

63. Access Point

64. To connect multiple devices and broadcast data

65. Sends data only to the intended recipient

66. Data packets travel in a predictable path

67. In networks requiring easy management and troubleshooting

68. Monitoring, maintaining, and optimizing network performance

69. To connect different networks and manage traffic

70. Switch

71. Enhancing security and reducing congestion

72. To protect the network by filtering unauthorized access

73. Mesh

74. By allowing multiple paths for data to travel

75. To monitor and identify potential security breaches

76. Bus

77. Secure remote access over the internet

78. It broadcasts data to all connected devices

79. More efficient data handling by sending data only to the intended recipient

80. Both speed and reliability of the network

81. Bus

82. Protecting both hardware and software from unauthorized access and attacks

83. To connect different networks and manage traffic

84. The maximum data transfer rate of the network

85. Data travels in one direction or both directions in a loop

86. By isolating problems within specific segments

87. To provide secure and encrypted communication over a public network

88. Increased reliability and fault

tolerance

89. Prioritization of critical network traffic

90. It filters and blocks unauthorized access

91. A mesh topology offers higher redundancy due to multiple connections between devices

92. Both speed and reliability of the network

93. Switch

94. Simplicity and low cost

95. By providing multiple paths for data to travel

96. To connect multiple devices and broadcast data to all

Chapter 3: Mastering Cryptography

3.1 History of Cryptography

Cryptography, the art of secure communication, has evolved significantly over millennia. Its origins trace back to ancient civilizations, where rudimentary methods were employed to safeguard messages. The earliest known use of cryptography was by the ancient Egyptians, who used simple substitution ciphers to encode their hieroglyphs. These early techniques laid the foundation for more complex systems. The Greeks further advanced cryptographic methods; one notable example is the use of the scytale, a tool used by the Spartans to encode messages by wrapping a strip of parchment around a cylindrical object.

During the medieval period, cryptography saw substantial developments with the advent of more sophisticated encryption techniques. The Arabic mathematician Al-Kindi is often credited with introducing frequency analysis, a groundbreaking method for breaking ciphers by studying the frequency of letters in the ciphertext. This period also witnessed the widespread use of the Vigenère cipher, a polyalphabetic substitution cipher that provided a significant leap in cryptographic security over simpler substitution methods.

The modern era of cryptography began with the advent of computers and electronic communication. The 20th century saw the development of advanced algorithms such as the Data Encryption Standard (DES) and the RSA algorithm, which form the backbone of contemporary cryptographic practices. The rise of public-key cryptography in the 1970s, exemplified by the RSA algorithm, marked a paradigm shift by allowing secure communications without the need for a shared secret key. Today, cryptography is integral to information security, with ongoing advancements ensuring the protection of digital communications and data against ever-evolving threats.

3.2 Encryption Algorithms

Encryption algorithms are fundamental to securing data, transforming plaintext into ciphertext to prevent unauthorized access. Various algorithms have been developed to meet different security needs, each with its unique strengths and applications. Below, we explore some of the most prominent encryption algorithms.

Data Encryption Standard (DES)

The Data Encryption Standard (DES) is one of the earliest and most well-known symmetric encryption algorithms. Developed by IBM in the 1970s and adopted by the U.S. National Institute of Standards and Technology (NIST) in 1977, DES uses a 56-bit key to encrypt 64-bit blocks of data. Despite its historical significance and widespread use, DES is now considered insecure due to its relatively short key length, which makes it vulnerable to brute-force attacks. It has largely been superseded by more robust algorithms, but its development was a critical milestone in cryptographic history.

Advanced Encryption Standard (AES)

The Advanced Encryption Standard (AES) was established as a successor to DES after a public competition organized by NIST. AES is a symmetric encryption algorithm that operates on block sizes of 128 bits, with key lengths of 128, 192, or 256 bits. AES is widely recognized for its security and efficiency and is used globally to protect sensitive data. Its design, which includes multiple rounds of substitution, permutation, and mixing operations, ensures strong encryption against various types of cryptographic attacks.

RSA Algorithm

The RSA algorithm, named after its inventors Rivest, Shamir, and Adleman, introduced the concept of public-key cryptography. Developed in 1977, RSA uses a pair of keys: a public key for encryption and a private key for decryption. This asymmetric encryption method relies on the difficulty of factoring large composite numbers into their prime factors. RSA is widely used for secure data transmission and digital signatures. Its robustness and versatility make it a cornerstone of modern cryptographic practices.

Elliptic Curve Cryptography (ECC)

Elliptic Curve Cryptography (ECC) is an asymmetric encryption technique based on the mathematics of elliptic curves. ECC offers similar levels of security to RSA but with shorter key lengths, making it more efficient in terms of computational resources and storage. This efficiency makes ECC particularly suitable for mobile and embedded devices with limited processing power. ECC has gained significant adoption in modern cryptographic systems, including secure messaging and digital signatures.

Blowfish

Blowfish is a symmetric key block cipher designed by Bruce Schneier in 1993. It operates on 64-bit blocks and supports key lengths ranging from 32 to 448 bits. Blowfish is known for its simplicity and speed, as well as its strong security features. Although newer algorithms like AES have become more prevalent, Blowfish remains a viable option for certain applications due to its flexibility and effectiveness. It has been widely used in various encryption protocols and software.

Twofish

Twofish is a successor to Blowfish, also designed by Bruce Schneier. It is a symmetric key block cipher that operates on 128-bit blocks and supports key lengths of up to 256 bits. Twofish is known for its high performance and security, utilizing a complex key schedule and multiple rounds of transformation to ensure robustness against attacks. While it did not become the standard encryption algorithm, Twofish is still used in various cryptographic systems and applications.

Each of these encryption algorithms has played a significant role in the evolution of cryptographic techniques, addressing different needs and security requirements in the ever-changing landscape of information security.

3.3   Public and Private Key Infrastructures

Public and private key infrastructures are critical components of modern cryptography, enabling secure communication and authentication. These infrastructures manage the use of cryptographic keys to protect data and verify identities. Understanding how these systems work is essential for implementing effective security measures.

Public Key Infrastructure (PKI)

Public Key Infrastructure (PKI) is a framework that uses asymmetric cryptography to provide security services such as encryption, decryption, and digital signatures. PKI relies on a pair of keys: a public key, which is widely distributed and used for encryption, and a private key, which is kept confidential and used for decryption. The key management process is supported by various entities within the PKI system:

- **Certificate Authorities (CAs)**: CAs issue digital certificates that validate the identity of entities and bind their public keys to their identities. These certificates are essential for establishing trust between communicating parties. - **Registration Authorities (RAs)**: RAs handle the process of verifying the identity of entities requesting digital certificates and pass this information to the CA. - **Certificate Revocation Lists (CRLs) and Online Certificate Status Protocol (OCSP)**: These mechanisms are used to manage and verify the status of certificates, ensuring that revoked or expired certificates are not used.

PKI is widely employed in various applications, including secure email, web transactions (HTTPS), and digital signatures. Its structure ensures that data can be securely encrypted and transmitted between parties who have no prior knowledge of each other, relying on trusted third parties for validation.

Private Key Infrastructure (PKI)

Private Key Infrastructure (often referred to as a private key system) operates differently from PKI, focusing on symmetric cryptography where a single key is used for both encryption and decryption. This key must be shared securely between parties to ensure that only authorized entities can access the encrypted information. Key aspects of **Private Key Infrastructure** include:

- **Key Distribution**: Since the same key is used for both encryption and decryption, secure key distribution is crucial. Techniques such as secure channels or key exchange algorithms are employed to ensure that keys are transmitted safely. - **Key Management**: Effective management practices are necessary to handle the lifecycle of symmetric keys, including their generation, storage, and rotation. Tools and protocols are used to maintain the security of these keys. - **Scalability Issues**: Unlike PKI, which scales effectively with the use of public and private key pairs, private key systems can face challenges as the number of participants grows. Each pair of communicating entities needs a unique key, leading to a complex key management scenario in large networks.

Private Key Infrastructure is often used in scenarios where speed and efficiency are critical, and where secure channels for key distribution are established. It is commonly utilized in systems where parties have an established relationship and can securely share and manage their symmetric keys.

Both **Public** and **Private Key Infrastructures** are vital for ensuring secure communication and data protection in various digital environments. Each system has its specific use cases, benefits, and challenges, and understanding both is crucial for implementing effective security solutions.

3.4 How to Embed Encryption in a Real Business Scenario

Embedding encryption into a real business scenario involves integrating cryptographic techniques into the organization's operations and systems to protect sensitive data. Effective implementation requires careful planning, execution, and ongoing management to ensure that data remains secure throughout its lifecycle.

First, businesses should start by identifying the types of data that require protection and the potential risks associated with their exposure. This includes sensitive customer information, financial records, intellectual property, and confidential communications. Once these data types are identified, businesses need to assess their current security posture and determine where encryption can be most effectively applied. For example, data at rest (such as files stored on servers) and data in transit (such as information sent over the internet) both require different encryption strategies. Implementing encryption solutions such as Full Disk Encryption (FDE) for data at rest and Transport Layer Security (TLS) for data in transit can mitigate risks and enhance data security.

Next, businesses need to select appropriate encryption technologies and tools based on their requirements. For instance, adopting symmetric encryption algorithms like Advanced Encryption Standard (AES) for encrypting large volumes of data can be efficient, while asymmetric algorithms like RSA can be used for securing key exchanges and digital signatures. It is also essential to consider how encryption will be integrated into existing systems and workflows. This may involve configuring encryption settings in software applications, databases, and communication protocols. Organizations must ensure that encryption practices do not interfere with business operations and that they provide a seamless user experience.

Finally, ongoing management and monitoring are crucial for maintaining encryption effectiveness. This includes regularly updating encryption algorithms to defend against evolving threats, managing encryption keys securely, and conducting periodic security audits. Businesses should also implement policies and training programs to educate employees about encryption best practices and the importance of safeguarding sensitive data. By embedding encryption into their business processes and infrastructure, organizations can protect their data, comply with regulatory requirements, and build trust with customers and partners.

Overall, embedding encryption requires a strategic approach, from assessing data security needs to selecting suitable technologies and ensuring proper management. By following these steps, businesses can effectively leverage encryption to enhance their data security and safeguard their operations against potential threats.

3.5 Quiz - Handle the Secrets of Cryptography

1. What does **cryptography** primarily ensure?

   ☐ Data compression
   ☐ Data accessibility
   ☐ Data confidentiality
   ☐ Data redundancy

2. What type of algorithm is **DES**?

   ☐ Symmetric key algorithm
   ☐ Asymmetric key algorithm
   ☐ Hash function
   ☐ Digital signature algorithm

3. The **RSA** algorithm uses which type of cryptography?

   ☐ Symmetric key cryptography
   ☐ Hash cryptography
   ☐ Asymmetric key cryptography
   ☐ Stream cipher cryptography

4. **AES** operates on blocks of what size?

   ☐ 64 bits
   ☐ 128 bits
   ☐ 256 bits
   ☐ 512 bits

5. What is a **Certificate Authority (CA)** responsible for?

   ☐ Encrypting data
   ☐ Issuing digital certificates
   ☐ Generating encryption keys
   ☐ Managing cryptographic algorithms

6. **Blowfish** is known for which of the following features?

   ☐ High computational complexity
   ☐ Variable key length
   ☐ Asymmetric encryption

☐ Large block size

7. **ECC** stands for what type of cryptography?

   ☐ Symmetric key cryptography
   ☐ Hash cryptography
   ☐ Elliptic Curve Cryptography
   ☐ Block cipher cryptography

8. The **Vigenère** cipher is an example of which type of encryption?

   ☐ Asymmetric encryption
   ☐ Hash function
   ☐ Polyalphabetic substitution
   ☐ Stream cipher

9. **Public key infrastructure (PKI)** involves which of the following?

   ☐ Shared keys
   ☐ Public and private keys
   ☐ Only private keys
   ☐ Symmetric encryption only

10. What is the main function of **frequency analysis** in cryptography?

    ☐ Encrypting messages
    ☐ Generating random numbers
    ☐ Breaking ciphers by analyzing letter frequency
    ☐ Secure key distribution

11. **Twofish** is a successor to which encryption algorithm?

    ☐ AES
    ☐ Blowfish
    ☐ DES
    ☐ RSA

12. What does **PKI** provide for data encryption?

    ☐ Only physical security
    ☐ Key management
    ☐ Symmetric encryption only

☐ Public key infrastructure for encryption and authentication

13. The primary purpose of **encryption keys** is to:

    ☐ Ensure high-speed data transfer
    ☐ Securely encode and decode data
    ☐ Manage network traffic
    ☐ Increase data redundancy

14. **AES** uses which type of encryption method?

    ☐ Asymmetric
    ☐ Symmetric
    ☐ Hashing
    ☐ Public-key

15. What is the role of a **Registration Authority (RA)** in PKI?

    ☐ Verify identities before issuing certificates
    ☐ Manage certificate revocation
    ☐ Encrypt messages
    ☐ Generate encryption keys

16. The **scytale** was used in which ancient encryption method?

    ☐ Transposition cipher
    ☐ Substitution cipher
    ☐ Modern cryptography
    ☐ Hashing function

17. **RSA** algorithm's security is based on the difficulty of:

    ☐ Solving linear equations
    ☐ Factoring large composite numbers
    ☐ Calculating prime numbers
    ☐ Breaking symmetric keys

18. What type of encryption is used in **Transport Layer Security (TLS)**?

    ☐ Symmetric and asymmetric encryption
    ☐ Only symmetric encryption

☐ Only asymmetric encryption
☐ Hashing only

19. In the context of cryptography, **digital signatures** are used for:

☐ Encrypting data only
☐ Generating random numbers
☐ Verifying the authenticity and integrity of a message
☐ Managing encryption keys

20. **Full Disk Encryption (FDE)** protects:

☐ Only network traffic
☐ Data in transit
☐ Data stored on a disk
☐ Email communications

21. **Hash functions** are used for:

☐ Encrypting data
☐ Producing a fixed-size output from variable-size input
☐ Generating symmetric keys
☐ Establishing secure communications

22. What is the main advantage of **Elliptic Curve Cryptography (ECC)**?

☐ Longer key lengths
☐ High security with shorter key lengths
☐ Simpler key management
☐ Faster encryption speeds

23. **Key Management** in a symmetric system includes:

☐ Key exchange only
☐ Key generation, distribution, and storage
☐ Certificate issuance
☐ Public key distribution

24. What does **frequency analysis** help to break?

☐ Symmetric keys

☐ Public key encryption
☐ Substitution ciphers
☐ Hash functions

25. **Cryptographic keys** are typically used to:

☐ Authenticate users
☐ Increase system performance
☐ Encrypt and decrypt data
☐ Manage network traffic

26. The **Caesar cipher** is an example of:

☐ Public key cryptography
☐ Hash functions
☐ Substitution cipher
☐ Elliptic curve encryption

27. **Secure key exchange** is crucial for:

☐ Data compression
☐ Public key distribution
☐ Symmetric encryption systems
☐ Digital signature verification

28. **Digital certificates** are used to:

☐ Verify identities and public keys
☐ Encrypt data directly
☐ Manage private keys
☐ Generate encryption algorithms

29. **HMAC** stands for:

☐ Hash-based Message Authentication Code
☐ Hypertext Message Authentication Code
☐ Hash-based Message Authentication Code
☐ Hash-based Multi Authentication Code

30. Which encryption method is **Blowfish**?

☐ Asymmetric

☐ Hashing
☐ Symmetric key
☐ Public key

31. **Digital signatures** are crucial for:

☐ Encrypting large data
☐ Increasing data redundancy
☐ Authenticating data and verifying integrity
☐ Managing encryption keys

32. The **SHA-256** algorithm is a type of:

☐ Symmetric encryption
☐ Asymmetric encryption
☐ Hash function
☐ Key exchange protocol

33. **Public key cryptography** is also known as:

☐ Symmetric encryption
☐ Asymmetric encryption
☐ Hashing
☐ Key management

34. **Elliptic Curve Cryptography (ECC)** is efficient because:

☐ It uses long key lengths
☐ It requires less computational power
☐ It provides high security with shorter key lengths
☐ It is easier to implement

35. What does **AES** stand for?

☐ Advanced Encryption Standard
☐ Advanced Encoding System
☐ Advanced Encryption Standard
☐ Applied Encryption Scheme

36. The **RC4** algorithm is classified as:

☐ A block cipher

☐ A stream cipher
☐ A hashing function
☐ An asymmetric encryption algorithm

37. **Cryptanalysis** involves:

☐ Creating new encryption algorithms
☐ Analyzing and breaking cryptographic systems
☐ Managing encryption keys
☐ Encrypting messages

38. Which of the following is NOT a common use of **cryptography**?

☐ Data encryption
☐ Digital signatures
☐ Secure key exchange
☐ Speeding up network traffic

39. The **Blowfish** cipher was designed by:

☐ Ron Rivest
☐ Adi Shamir
☐ Bruce Schneier
☐ Whitfield Diffie

40. **Digital signatures** help to ensure:

☐ Fast data transfer
☐ Redundancy of data
☐ Data authenticity and integrity
☐ Data compression

41. Which encryption standard uses a key size of 256 bits by default?

☐ DES
☐ Blowfish
☐ AES
☐ RSA

42. The **RSA** algorithm is primarily used for:

☐ Symmetric encryption

☐ Hashing
☐ Public-key encryption
☐ Stream ciphers

43. **Key pairs** in asymmetric cryptography consist of:

☐ Two identical keys
☐ A key and a salt
☐ A public key and a private key
☐ Two public keys

44. The primary use of **cryptographic hashing functions** is to:

☐ Encrypt data
☐ Exchange keys
☐ Verify data integrity
☐ Generate encryption keys

45. Which of the following is a symmetric encryption algorithm?

☐ RSA
☐ ECC
☐ AES
☐ SHA-256

46. **TLS** is used to secure:

☐ Data storage
☐ Data in transit over networks
☐ Disk encryption
☐ Data compression

47. **Public key encryption** is used primarily for:

☐ Speeding up encryption
☐ Secure key exchange and digital signatures
☐ Compressing data
☐ Encrypting large files

48. The **Caesar cipher** is an example of:

☐ Substitution cipher

☐ Transposition cipher
☐ Hash function
☐ Stream cipher

49. In cryptography, a **cipher** refers to:

☐ A type of key
☐ An algorithm for encryption and decryption
☐ A secure communication channel
☐ A data integrity check

50. **AES** is classified as:

☐ A hash function
☐ An asymmetric encryption algorithm
☐ A symmetric encryption algorithm
☐ A public key algorithm

51. **Digital certificates** are used in:

☐ Key exchange
☐ Symmetric encryption
☐ Authenticating identities
☐ Hashing functions

52. The **Diffie-Hellman** algorithm is used for:

☐ Symmetric encryption
☐ Secure key exchange
☐ Hashing data
☐ Digital signatures

53. **AES** supports key sizes of:

☐ 64, 128, and 256 bits
☐ 128 and 512 bits
☐ 128, 192, and 256 bits
☐ 64 and 256 bits

54. **ECC** is popular for its:

☐ Long key lengths

☐ High computational requirements
☐ High security with short key lengths
☐ High speed in decryption

55. **SHA-1** is a type of:

☐ Symmetric encryption algorithm
☐ Public key algorithm
☐ Hash function
☐ Digital signature algorithm

56. **PGP** stands for:

☐ Pretty Good Privacy
☐ Public Good Protocol
☐ Pretty Good Privacy
☐ Public Generic Protocol

57. Which of the following is NOT a type of encryption algorithm?

☐ DES
☐ AES
☐ RSA
☐ URL encoding

58. The **HMAC** algorithm is used for:

☐ Key generation
☐ Public key encryption
☐ Message authentication
☐ Data compression

59. **Blowfish** is designed to replace:

☐ RSA
☐ AES
☐ DES
☐ ECC

60. **RSA** encryption involves:

☐ Hashing data

☐ Symmetric encryption
☐ Asymmetric key pairs
☐ Data compression

61. **Public key encryption** is known for:

☐ Speed
☐ Simplicity
☐ Key pairs
☐ Data redundancy

62. What is the main characteristic of **hash functions**?

☐ They can be reversed
☐ They encrypt data
☐ They produce a fixed-size output
☐ They use variable-length keys

63. The **DES** algorithm is based on:

☐ Elliptic curves
☐ Public key infrastructure
☐ Symmetric key encryption
☐ Hashing functions

64. **Cryptographic key exchange** methods are essential for:

☐ Data integrity
☐ Speed optimization
☐ Establishing shared keys securely
☐ Data encryption

65. **Elliptic Curve Cryptography** is known for:

☐ Its use of long keys
☐ Its reliance on symmetric keys
☐ Its efficiency with shorter key lengths
☐ Its simplicity in design

66. What is the function of a **ciphertext**?

☐ Encrypting data

- ☐ Generating keys
- ☐ The encrypted output of plaintext
- ☐ Managing public keys

67. **SHA-2** is:

- ☐ A family of cryptographic hash functions
- ☐ An encryption algorithm
- ☐ A key exchange protocol
- ☐ A symmetric cipher

68. **Key length** in encryption affects:

- ☐ The speed of encryption
- ☐ The ease of key management
- ☐ The security level of the encryption
- ☐ The data compression ratio

69. **Digital certificates** are used in:

- ☐ Secure communications and identity verification
- ☐ Data compression
- ☐ Key management
- ☐ Speeding up encryption

70. The main feature of **ECC** is:

- ☐ High computational complexity
- ☐ Long key lengths
- ☐ High security with smaller key sizes
- ☐ High speed in encryption

71. The **ElGamal** encryption algorithm is used for:

- ☐ Hashing
- ☐ Public key encryption
- ☐ Symmetric encryption
- ☐ Key management

72. **DES** was replaced by **AES** because:

- ☐ DES was too fast

□ DES had a short key length and was less secure
□ AES was cheaper
□ DES used modern techniques

73. The **Kasiski examination** is used for:

□ Breaking Vigenère ciphers
□ Encrypting data
□ Key management
□ Hashing functions

74. **HMAC** uses which type of cryptography?

□ Symmetric key cryptography
□ Asymmetric key cryptography
□ Public key infrastructure
□ Hashing only

75. The **IDEA** cipher is a:

□ Hash function
□ Asymmetric algorithm
□ Symmetric key algorithm
□ Digital signature algorithm

76. **Public key infrastructure (PKI)** is important for:

□ Key management
□ Data compression
□ Managing digital certificates and encryption keys
□ Speeding up encryption

77. **RSA** is known for its:

□ Symmetric encryption
□ Asymmetric encryption
□ Hash functions
□ Data compression

78. **Key exchange protocols** are used to:

□ Encrypt data

☐ Securely share keys over an insecure channel
☐ Create digital signatures
☐ Manage encryption algorithms

79. **DES** stands for:

☐ Data Encryption Standard
☐ Digital Encoding Scheme
☐ Data Encryption Standard
☐ Dynamic Encryption System

80. The **Vigenère cipher** is an example of a:

☐ Substitution cipher
☐ Polyalphabetic cipher
☐ Transposition cipher
☐ Hash function

81. **SHA-256** is a member of which family?

☐ SHA-2
☐ SHA-1
☐ SHA-3
☐ MD5

3.6 Answers to The Questions

Great! Now, check your answer:

1. Data confidentiality

2. Symmetric key algorithm

3. Asymmetric key cryptography

4. 128 bits

5. Issuing digital certificates

6. Variable key length

7. Elliptic Curve Cryptography

8. Polyalphabetic substitution

9. Public and private keys

10. Breaking ciphers by analyzing letter frequency

11. Blowfish

12. Public key infrastructure for encryption and authentication

13. Securely encode and decode data

14. Symmetric

15. Verify identities before issuing certificates

16. Transposition cipher

17. Factoring large composite numbers

18. Symmetric and asymmetric encryption

19. Verifying the authenticity and integrity of a message

20. Data stored on a disk

21. Producing a fixed-size output from variable-size input

22. High security with shorter key lengths

23. Key generation, distribution, and storage

24. Substitution ciphers

25. Encrypt and decrypt data

26. Substitution cipher

27. Symmetric encryption systems

28. Verify identities and public keys

29. Hash-based Message Authentication Code

30. Symmetric key

31. Authenticating data and verifying integrity

32. Hash function

33. Asymmetric encryption

34. It provides high security with shorter key lengths

35. Advanced Encryption Standard

36. A stream cipher

37. Analyzing and breaking cryptographic systems

38. Speeding up network traffic

39. Bruce Schneier

40. Data authenticity and integrity

41. AES

42. Public-key encryption

43. A public key and a private key

44. Verify data integrity

45. AES

46. Data in transit over networks

47. Secure key exchange and digital signatures

48. Substitution cipher

49. An algorithm for encryption and decryption

50. A symmetric encryption algorithm

51. Authenticating identities

52. Secure key exchange

53. 128, 192, and 256 bits

54. High security with short key lengths

55. Hash function

56. Pretty Good Privacy

57. URL encoding

58. Message authentication

59. DES

60. Asymmetric key pairs

61. Key pairs

62. They produce a fixed-size output

63. Symmetric key encryption

64. Establishing shared keys securely

65. Its efficiency with shorter key lengths

66. The encrypted output of plaintext

67. A family of cryptographic hash functions

68. The security level of the encryption

69. Secure communications and identity verification

70. High security with smaller key sizes

71. Public key encryption

72. DES had a short key length and was less secure

73. Breaking Vigenère ciphers

74. Symmetric key cryptography

75. Symmetric key algorithm

76. Managing digital certificates and encryption keys

77. Asymmetric encryption

78. Securely share keys over an insecure channel

79. Data Encryption Standard

80. Polyalphabetic cipher

81. SHA-2

Chapter 4: Identity and Access Management

4.1 Introduction to Identity and Access Management

Identity and Access Management (IAM) is a critical component of modern cybersecurity practices. It involves the processes and technologies used to manage and secure digital identities and control access to various resources within an organization. IAM ensures that the right individuals have the appropriate access to technology resources at the right times and for the right reasons. This includes managing user identities, authentication methods, and access controls to safeguard sensitive information and systems from unauthorized access.

In today's digital landscape, where data breaches and cyber-attacks are prevalent, effective IAM is essential for maintaining organizational security and compliance. IAM systems help organizations enforce security policies, manage user credentials, and monitor access activities. By implementing robust IAM practices, businesses can protect their assets, reduce risks associated with unauthorized access, and ensure that compliance requirements are met.

4.2 Core Concepts of IAM

Identity Management

Identity management refers to the creation, maintenance, and deletion of user identities within an organization. This process includes assigning unique identifiers to users, such as usernames or IDs, and managing their associated attributes and roles. Effective identity management ensures that each user has a unique and verified identity, which is crucial for tracking and controlling access to systems and data.

Key components of identity management include user provisioning, de-provisioning, and maintaining up-to-date identity records. User provisioning involves creating new accounts and assigning appropriate roles and permissions. De-provisioning, on the other hand, involves removing or disabling accounts when users leave the organization or no longer require access. Maintaining accurate and up-to-date identity records helps prevent security vulnerabilities associated with orphaned or outdated accounts.

Authentication Methods

Authentication is the process of verifying the identity of a user before granting access to resources. Various authentication methods are used to confirm that users are who they claim to be. These methods can be broadly categorized into single-factor authentication (SFA) and multi-factor authentication (MFA).

Single-factor authentication relies on one type of credential, such as a password or PIN, to verify a user's identity. While SFA is simple and widely used, it is less secure compared to MFA. Multi-factor authentication requires users to provide two or more forms of identification, typically involving something they know (e.g., a password), something they have (e.g., a smartphone or security token), or something they are (e.g., a fingerprint). MFA significantly enhances security by adding additional layers of verification, making it more challenging for unauthorized individuals to gain access.

Access Control Models

Access control models define the policies and mechanisms used to regulate access to resources within an organization. These models are essential for implementing security policies and ensuring that users have the appropriate level of access based on their roles and responsibilities.

Three primary access control models are commonly used:

- **Discretionary Access Control (DAC):** In DAC, resource owners have the authority to grant or deny access to their resources. Users can share access with others based on their discretion. While DAC offers flexibility, it can be challenging to manage and enforce consistent access policies.
- **Mandatory Access Control (MAC):** MAC enforces access policies

based on predefined security labels or classifications assigned to both users and resources. Users are granted access based on these labels, and access decisions are made by the system based on policy rules. MAC provides a higher level of control and is often used in environments requiring strict security measures.

- **Role-Based Access Control (RBAC):** RBAC assigns access permissions based on user roles within an organization. Each role has specific permissions associated with it, and users are assigned to roles based on their job functions. RBAC simplifies access management by grouping users into roles and defining permissions at the role level.

4.3 Implementing IAM Solutions

IAM Policies and Procedures

Effective IAM implementation requires establishing comprehensive policies and procedures to guide identity and access management activities. IAM policies outline the rules and guidelines for managing user identities, authentication methods, and access controls. These policies should address aspects such as user provisioning, password management, access request processes, and periodic reviews of access permissions.

Procedures for managing IAM should include steps for onboarding new users, updating user roles and permissions, and handling access requests and approvals. Regular audits and reviews of IAM policies and procedures help ensure compliance with organizational standards and regulatory requirements, identify potential security gaps, and improve overall IAM effectiveness.

IAM Technologies and Tools

Various technologies and tools are available to support IAM efforts and enhance security. These include:

- **Identity Management Systems:** These systems provide centralized management of user identities and attributes, streamlining processes such as user provisioning, de-provisioning, and role management.
- **Single Sign-On (SSO):** SSO solutions enable users to authenticate once and gain access to multiple applications or systems without

needing to log in separately for each one. This improves user convenience and reduces the risk of password fatigue.

- **Identity Federation:** Federation allows organizations to extend authentication and authorization capabilities across different domains or organizations, enabling users to access resources in external systems using their existing credentials.
- **Multi-Factor Authentication (MFA):** MFA solutions add an extra layer of security by requiring users to provide multiple forms of verification before granting access. This reduces the risk of unauthorized access due to compromised credentials.
- **Access Management Solutions:** These tools help enforce access policies, monitor user activities, and manage permissions based on roles and responsibilities.

Best Practices for IAM

To ensure effective and secure IAM implementation, organizations should follow best practices, including:

- **Regularly Review and Update Access Permissions:** Periodic reviews of user access permissions help ensure that users have appropriate access levels based on their current roles and responsibilities.
- **Enforce Strong Authentication Methods:** Implement MFA and strong password policies to enhance security and protect against unauthorized access.
- **Monitor and Audit IAM Activities:** Continuously monitor and audit IAM activities to detect and respond to suspicious behaviors, potential security incidents, and compliance issues.
- **Implement Least Privilege Principle:** Grant users only the minimum level of access necessary to perform their job functions, reducing the risk of unauthorized access or accidental data exposure.
- **Educate Users About Security Best Practices:** Provide training and awareness programs to educate users about security policies, proper handling of credentials, and recognizing phishing attempts.

4.4 Quiz: Identity and Access Management

1. **What does IAM stand for?**

   ☐ Integrated Access Management
   ☐ Identity and Access Management
   ☐ Internet and Account Management
   ☐ Identity and Application Monitoring

2. **Which of the following is a core component of IAM?**

   ☐ Data encryption
   ☐ Firewall rules
   ☐ Identity management
   ☐ Network monitoring

3. **What is the main purpose of authentication in IAM?**

   ☐ To verify the identity of users
   ☐ To manage user roles
   ☐ To track network traffic
   ☐ To encrypt data

4. **Which authentication method requires multiple forms of identification?**

   ☐ Single-factor authentication
   ☐ Multi-factor authentication
   ☐ Biometric authentication
   ☐ Password-based authentication

5. **What does RBAC stand for?**

   ☐ Role-Based Access Control
   ☐ Role-Based Access Control
   ☐ Restricted Business Access Control
   ☐ Remote-Based Authentication Control

6. **What is the primary benefit of using Role-Based Access Control (RBAC)?**

   ☐ Simplifies password management

☐ Enhances encryption algorithms
☐ Simplifies access management by roles
☐ Increases network bandwidth

7. **What does DAC stand for in access control models?**

☐ Discretionary Access Control
☐ Data Access Control
☐ Direct Access Control
☐ Dynamic Access Control

8. **Which access control model enforces access based on predefined security labels?**

☐ Discretionary Access Control (DAC)
☐ Role-Based Access Control (RBAC)
☐ Mandatory Access Control (MAC)
☐ Attribute-Based Access Control (ABAC)

9. **What is the primary function of identity management?**

☐ Creating and maintaining user identities
☐ Encrypting sensitive data
☐ Monitoring network traffic
☐ Implementing firewall rules

10. **Which technology allows users to authenticate once and access multiple systems?**

☐ Identity Federation
☐ Single Sign-On (SSO)
☐ Multi-Factor Authentication (MFA)
☐ Public Key Infrastructure (PKI)

11. **Which component is essential for managing digital certificates and encryption keys?**

☐ Key Management System
☐ Public Key Infrastructure (PKI)
☐ Single Sign-On (SSO)
☐ Multi-Factor Authentication (MFA)

12. **What is the purpose of user provisioning in IAM?**

   ☐ To manage encryption keys
   ☐ To create and assign user accounts and permissions
   ☐ To monitor network traffic
   ☐ To enforce access control policies

13. **Which authentication method involves something the user is, such as a fingerprint?**

   ☐ Single-factor authentication
   ☐ Multi-factor authentication
   ☐ Biometric authentication
   ☐ Token-based authentication

14. **What is the main characteristic of Mandatory Access Control (MAC)?**

   ☐ It allows resource owners to control access
   ☐ It relies on user roles for access decisions
   ☐ It enforces access based on security labels and policy rules
   ☐ It simplifies password management

15. **Which access control model is known for being highly flexible but potentially difficult to manage?**

   ☐ Mandatory Access Control (MAC)
   ☐ Role-Based Access Control (RBAC)
   ☐ Discretionary Access Control (DAC)
   ☐ Attribute-Based Access Control (ABAC)

16. **Which IAM practice involves removing access rights when a user leaves the organization?**

   ☐ User provisioning
   ☐ User de-provisioning
   ☐ Role management
   ☐ Access auditing

17. **What does the Least Privilege Principle dictate?**

   ☐ Users should have the highest level of access necessary

☐ Users should have access to all data and systems
☐ Users should have the minimum level of access necessary for their role
☐ Users should only have access to public data

18. **Which technology helps in extending authentication across different domains or organizations?**

☐ Multi-Factor Authentication (MFA)
☐ Single Sign-On (SSO)
☐ Identity Federation
☐ Token-Based Authentication

19. **What is the key benefit of implementing Multi-Factor Authentication (MFA)?**

☐ Simplifies password management
☐ Reduces the number of required passwords
☐ Enhances security by requiring multiple forms of verification
☐ Increases network bandwidth

20. **Which IAM technology provides centralized management of user identities and attributes?**

☐ Single Sign-On (SSO)
☐ Multi-Factor Authentication (MFA)
☐ Identity Management Systems
☐ Public Key Infrastructure (PKI)

21. **What does Identity Federation enable?**

☐ Access to resources in external systems using existing credentials
☐ Encryption of sensitive data
☐ Monitoring of user activities
☐ Creation of user accounts and roles

22. **Which practice involves ensuring users have appropriate access based on their current job roles?**

☐ User provisioning
☐ Password management

☐ Access review and management
☐ Role assignment

23. **What is a primary function of an IAM system in relation to security policies?**

☐ To monitor network traffic
☐ To enforce and manage security policies related to access
☐ To encrypt sensitive data
☐ To manage firewall rules

24. **What is a key characteristic of Role-Based Access Control (RBAC)?**

☐ It requires users to authenticate using biometrics
☐ It enforces access based on security labels
☐ It assigns permissions based on user roles
☐ It provides single sign-on capabilities

25. **Which IAM process involves the setup of new user accounts and the assignment of permissions?**

☐ User provisioning
☐ Access auditing
☐ Role management
☐ User de-provisioning

26. **What type of authentication involves using something the user has, like a security token?**

☐ Biometric authentication
☐ Single-factor authentication
☐ Token-based authentication
☐ Password-based authentication

27. **Which access control model allows the owner of a resource to decide who can access it?**

☐ Discretionary Access Control (DAC)
☐ Mandatory Access Control (MAC)
☐ Role-Based Access Control (RBAC)
☐ Attribute-Based Access Control (ABAC)

28. **Which best practice involves limiting user access to only what is necessary for their role?**

   ☐ Access monitoring
   ☐ Password policy enforcement
   ☐ Least privilege principle
   ☐ Network segmentation

29. **Which IAM component is responsible for managing and verifying digital certificates?**

   ☐ Single Sign-On (SSO)
   ☐ Public Key Infrastructure (PKI)
   ☐ Multi-Factor Authentication (MFA)
   ☐ Identity Federation

30. **Which access control model is often used in environments with strict security requirements?**

   ☐ Discretionary Access Control (DAC)
   ☐ Mandatory Access Control (MAC)
   ☐ Role-Based Access Control (RBAC)
   ☐ Attribute-Based Access Control (ABAC)

31. **Which technology allows users to access multiple systems using a single set of credentials?**

   ☐ Single Sign-On (SSO)
   ☐ Identity Federation
   ☐ Multi-Factor Authentication (MFA)
   ☐ Public Key Infrastructure (PKI)

32. **Which process is crucial for removing access rights when users no longer need them?**

   ☐ User provisioning
   ☐ User de-provisioning
   ☐ Role management
   ☐ Access auditing

33. **What does the term "Identity Federation" refer to?**

- ☐ Centralized management of user credentials
- ☐ Multi-Factor Authentication (MFA)
- ☐ Extending authentication across different domains
- ☐ User provisioning and de-provisioning

34. What does the Least Privilege Principle aim to achieve?

- ☐ Minimizes user access to only what is necessary
- ☐ Maximizes user access to all systems
- ☐ Ensures users can access data from any device
- ☐ Increases user privileges for administrative tasks

35. Which IAM technology helps in managing access permissions based on roles?

- ☐ Public Key Infrastructure (PKI)
- ☐ Multi-Factor Authentication (MFA)
- ☐ Role-Based Access Control (RBAC)
- ☐ Single Sign-On (SSO)

36. Which IAM component deals with creating and managing user accounts and permissions?

- ☐ Identity Management Systems
- ☐ Network Monitoring Tools
- ☐ Data Encryption Solutions
- ☐ Firewall Management Systems

37. Which practice involves reviewing and updating user access permissions regularly?

- ☐ User provisioning
- ☐ Password management
- ☐ Access review and management
- ☐ Network segmentation

38. Which technology enhances security by requiring additional verification methods?

- ☐ Single Sign-On (SSO)
- ☐ Public Key Infrastructure (PKI)
- ☐ Multi-Factor Authentication (MFA)

☐ Role-Based Access Control (RBAC)

39. **What does Single Sign-On (SSO) primarily aim to achieve?**

☐ Reduce the number of required passwords
☐ Allow users to access multiple systems with one set of credentials
☐ Encrypt user data
☐ Monitor user activities

40. **Which IAM component helps ensure that users have the minimum necessary access to perform their job?**

☐ Identity Federation
☐ Public Key Infrastructure (PKI)
☐ Least Privilege Principle
☐ Multi-Factor Authentication (MFA)

4.5 Answers to The Questions

Great! Now, check your answers:

1. Identity and Access Management

2. Identity management

3. To verify the identity of users

4. Multi-factor authentication

5. Role-Based Access Control

6. Simplifies access management by roles

7. Discretionary Access Control

8. Mandatory Access Control (MAC)

9. Creating and maintaining user identities

10. Single Sign-On (SSO)

11. Public Key Infrastructure (PKI)

12. To create and assign user accounts and permissions

13. Biometric authentication

14. It enforces access based on security labels and policy rules

15. Discretionary Access Control (DAC)

16. User de-provisioning

17. Users should have the minimum level of access necessary for their role

18. Identity Federation

19. Enhances security by requiring multiple forms of verification

20. Identity Management Systems

21. Access to resources in external systems using existing credentials

22. Access review and management

23. To enforce and manage security policies related to access

24. It assigns permissions based on user roles

25. User provisioning

26. Token-based authentication

27. Discretionary Access Control (DAC)

28. Least privilege principle

29. Public Key Infrastructure (PKI)

30. Mandatory Access Control (MAC)

31. Single Sign-On (SSO)

32. User de-provisioning

33. Extending authentication across different domains

34. Minimizes user access to only what is necessary

35. Role-Based Access Control (RBAC)

36. Identity Management Systems

37. Access review and management

38. Multi-Factor Authentication (MFA)

39. Allow users to access multiple systems with one set of credentials

40. Least Privilege Principle

Chapter 5: Risk Management

5.1 Introduction to Risk Management

Risk management is a crucial component of organizational strategy that involves identifying, assessing, and mitigating risks to ensure the continuity and success of an organization. It is a systematic approach to managing potential events or conditions that could negatively impact the organization's assets, operations, or objectives. Effective risk management helps organizations to anticipate potential threats, minimize adverse impacts, and capitalize on opportunities.

In the context of cybersecurity, risk management is particularly important as it addresses the vulnerabilities and threats that could compromise the integrity, availability, and confidentiality of information systems. By understanding and managing these risks, organizations can protect their digital assets from a range of potential threats, including cyberattacks, data breaches, and system failures.

5.2 Principles of Risk Management

Risk management is based on several key principles that guide the identification, assessment, and mitigation of risks. These principles include:

Risk Identification: This involves recognizing and documenting potential risks that could impact the organization. It is essential to consider various sources of risk, including internal processes, external threats, and technological vulnerabilities.

Risk Assessment: Once risks are identified, they need to be evaluated to determine their potential impact and likelihood. Risk assessment helps in prioritizing risks based on their severity and probability, allowing organizations to focus on the most critical threats.

Risk Mitigation: This principle involves developing and implementing strategies to reduce or eliminate identified risks. Risk mitigation may include implementing security controls, developing contingency plans, and adopting preventive measures.

Continuous Monitoring and Review: Risk management is an ongoing process that requires continuous monitoring and periodic reviews. Organizations must regularly assess their risk environment, evaluate the effectiveness of their risk management strategies, and make necessary adjustments to address emerging threats.

5.3   The Risk Management Process

The risk management process involves several steps that ensure a structured approach to managing risks. These steps include:

1. Risk Identification

The first step in the risk management process is identifying potential risks. This involves conducting a thorough analysis of the organization's environment, operations, and external factors to uncover risks that could affect its objectives. Techniques for risk identification include brainstorming sessions, risk assessments, and reviewing historical data.

2. Risk Assessment

After identifying risks, the next step is to assess their potential impact and likelihood. Risk assessment involves evaluating the severity of each risk and the probability of its occurrence. Tools such as risk matrices and probability-impact charts can help in quantifying and prioritizing risks based on their significance.

3. Risk Mitigation

Once risks are assessed, organizations need to develop strategies to mitigate them. Risk mitigation strategies can include implementing security controls, developing contingency plans, and adopting risk avoidance measures. The goal is to reduce the likelihood and impact of risks to an acceptable level.

4. Risk Monitoring

Risk monitoring involves continuously tracking the risk environment and assessing the effectiveness of mitigation strategies. This step ensures that risks are managed proactively and that any changes in the risk landscape are addressed promptly. Regular risk reviews and audits help in maintaining an effective risk management framework.

5. Risk Communication

Effective communication is essential for successful risk management. Organizations must ensure that stakeholders are informed about identified risks, mitigation strategies, and changes in the risk environment. Clear communication helps in aligning risk management efforts and ensuring that everyone is aware of their roles and responsibilities.

5.4   Risk Management Strategies

Several strategies can be employed to manage risks effectively. These strategies include:

Risk Avoidance

Risk avoidance involves altering plans or processes to eliminate the risk entirely. This strategy is often used when the potential impact of a risk is too severe or when there is a feasible alternative that avoids the risk altogether.

Risk Reduction

Risk reduction focuses on minimizing the likelihood or impact of a risk. This can be achieved through implementing security controls, improving processes, and enhancing safeguards to reduce the probability of the risk occurring or its impact if it does occur.

Risk Transfer

Risk transfer involves shifting the responsibility for managing a risk to another party. This can be done through contracts, insurance policies, or outsourcing arrangements. By transferring risk, organizations can mitigate potential financial losses and other consequences associated with the risk.

Risk Acceptance

Risk acceptance involves acknowledging the presence of a risk and deciding to live with it. This strategy is often used when the cost of mitigation is higher than the potential impact of the risk or when the risk is deemed acceptable based on the organization's risk tolerance.

5.5 Implementing Risk Management in an Organization

Implementing risk management effectively requires a structured approach and the involvement of key stakeholders. The following steps can help in establishing a robust risk management framework:

1. Establish a Risk Management Framework

Organizations should develop a risk management framework that outlines the processes, policies, and procedures for managing risks. This framework should define the roles and responsibilities of stakeholders, establish risk management objectives, and set guidelines for risk assessment and mitigation.

2. Develop Risk Management Policies

Policies and procedures should be developed to guide risk management activities. These policies should cover risk identification, assessment, mitigation, monitoring, and communication. Clear policies ensure that risk management practices are consistent and aligned with organizational objectives.

3. Train and Educate Employees

Training and education are essential for ensuring that employees understand their roles in the risk management process. Regular training sessions should be conducted to raise awareness about potential risks, mitigation strategies, and best practices for managing risks effectively.

5.6 Quiz: The Risk Management Strategies

1. What is the primary goal of risk management in cybersecurity?

   - ☐ To eliminate all risks completely
   - ☐ To identify, assess, and mitigate risks to protect assets
   - ☐ To reduce the cost of cybersecurity tools
   - ☐ To ensure compliance with regulations only

2. Which principle involves recognizing and documenting potential risks?

   - ☐ Risk assessment
   - ☐ Risk mitigation
   - ☐ Risk identification
   - ☐ Risk communication

3. In the risk management process, what follows risk identification?

   - ☐ Risk mitigation
   - ☐ Risk monitoring
   - ☐ Risk assessment
   - ☐ Risk communication

4. Which strategy involves reducing the likelihood or impact of a risk?

   - ☐ Risk avoidance
   - ☐ Risk reduction
   - ☐ Risk transfer
   - ☐ Risk acceptance

5. What is the purpose of risk monitoring in the risk management process?

   - ☐ To continuously track and assess risk management effectiveness
   - ☐ To identify new risks only
   - ☐ To eliminate risks completely
   - ☐ To review financial impacts only

6. Which risk management strategy involves shifting the

responsibility to another party?

- ☐ Risk avoidance
- ☐ Risk reduction
- ☐ Risk transfer
- ☐ Risk acceptance

7. **What does the Least Privilege Principle aim to achieve?**

- ☐ Maximizes user access to all systems
- ☐ Minimizes user access to only what is necessary
- ☐ Ensures users can access data from any device
- ☐ Increases user privileges for administrative tasks

8. **What does risk acceptance involve?**

- ☐ Acknowledging a risk and deciding to live with it
- ☐ Eliminating the risk completely
- ☐ Shifting the risk to another party
- ☐ Reducing the impact of the risk

9. **Which process involves creating and assigning user accounts, roles, and permissions?**

- ☐ Risk assessment
- ☐ User provisioning
- ☐ Risk monitoring
- ☐ Risk communication

10. **Which risk management strategy involves avoiding the risk entirely?**

- ☐ Risk avoidance
- ☐ Risk reduction
- ☐ Risk transfer
- ☐ Risk acceptance

11. **What is the role of risk communication in risk management?**

- ☐ To track and monitor risks continuously
- ☐ To identify new risks
- ☐ To inform stakeholders about risks and mitigation strategies

☐ To eliminate risks

12. **Which of the following is NOT a principle of risk management?**

   ☐ Risk identification
   ☐ Risk assessment
   ☐ Risk elimination
   ☐ Risk mitigation

13. **Which risk management component deals with evaluating the severity of risks?**

   ☐ Risk identification
   ☐ Risk assessment
   ☐ Risk transfer
   ☐ Risk avoidance

14. **What does risk reduction focus on?**

   ☐ Eliminating the risk
   ☐ Accepting the risk
   ☐ Minimizing the likelihood or impact of the risk
   ☐ Shifting the risk responsibility

15. **Which risk management strategy involves managing risks through insurance or contracts?**

   ☐ Risk avoidance
   ☐ Risk reduction
   ☐ Risk transfer
   ☐ Risk acceptance

16. **What is the primary focus of risk management in cybersecurity?**

   ☐ Enhancing physical security measures
   ☐ Managing employee benefits
   ☐ Protecting information systems from potential threats
   ☐ Reducing operational costs

17. **What is the first step in the risk management process?**

   ☐ Risk identification

- ☐ Risk assessment
- ☐ Risk mitigation
- ☐ Risk communication

18. **Which process involves continuously tracking the risk environment?**

    - ☐ Risk identification
    - ☐ Risk assessment
    - ☐ Risk monitoring
    - ☐ Risk communication

19. **Which strategy is used when the cost of mitigation exceeds the risk's potential impact?**

    - ☐ Risk avoidance
    - ☐ Risk reduction
    - ☐ Risk transfer
    - ☐ Risk acceptance

20. **What does a risk management framework outline?**

    - ☐ Security measures for physical threats
    - ☐ Financial policies for the organization
    - ☐ Processes, policies, and procedures for managing risks
    - ☐ Organizational hierarchy

21. **What role does training and education play in risk management?**

    - ☐ It helps in identifying new risks
    - ☐ It ensures employees understand their roles in risk management
    - ☐ It monitors risk management effectiveness
    - ☐ It develops risk communication strategies

22. **Which practice involves reviewing and updating user access permissions regularly?**

    - ☐ Risk assessment
    - ☐ Access review and management
    - ☐ Risk mitigation
    - ☐ Risk communication

23. **Which risk management strategy is often used to avoid potential risks by changing plans or processes?**

    ☐ Risk reduction
    ☐ Risk transfer
    ☐ Risk avoidance
    ☐ Risk acceptance

24. **Which component of risk management involves creating and implementing security controls?**

    ☐ Risk assessment
    ☐ Risk mitigation
    ☐ Risk monitoring
    ☐ Risk communication

25. **What is the purpose of a risk management policy?**

    ☐ To monitor and review risks
    ☐ To train employees
    ☐ To guide risk management activities and practices
    ☐ To identify new risks

26. **Which of the following is a key principle of risk management?**

    ☐ Risk elimination
    ☐ Risk identification
    ☐ Risk prevention
    ☐ Risk communication

27. **What is the main objective of risk reduction?**

    ☐ To eliminate all risks
    ☐ To minimize the likelihood or impact of a risk
    ☐ To transfer risks to another party
    ☐ To accept the risk

28. **Which document helps in setting guidelines for risk management practices?**

    ☐ Risk assessment report
    ☐ Risk communication plan

☐ Risk management policy
☐ Risk mitigation plan

29. **Which strategy involves managing a risk by implementing insurance or outsourcing?**

☐ Risk avoidance
☐ Risk reduction
☐ Risk transfer
☐ Risk acceptance

30. **What does risk assessment involve?**

☐ Developing risk mitigation strategies
☐ Identifying new risks
☐ Evaluating the severity and likelihood of risks
☐ Monitoring risk management effectiveness

31. **Which process is essential for tracking and responding to emerging risks?**

☐ Risk identification
☐ Risk assessment
☐ Risk monitoring
☐ Risk communication

32. **What is a primary benefit of implementing a risk management framework?**

☐ Reducing cybersecurity costs
☐ Improving employee productivity
☐ Protecting the organization's assets and objectives
☐ Enhancing physical security

33. **Which principle of risk management focuses on reducing risks to an acceptable level?**

☐ Risk transfer
☐ Risk avoidance
☐ Risk reduction
☐ Risk acceptance

34. **Which of the following is an example of a risk mitigation strategy?**

- ☐ Ignoring the risk
- ☐ Accepting the risk
- ☐ Implementing security controls
- ☐ Transferring the risk

35. **What role does a risk management framework play in an organization?**

- ☐ It trains employees on security best practices
- ☐ It monitors financial performance
- ☐ It provides a structured approach to managing risks
- ☐ It eliminates all potential risks

36. **Which component involves evaluating the impact of risks on the organization?**

- ☐ Risk identification
- ☐ Risk communication
- ☐ Risk assessment
- ☐ Risk mitigation

37. **Which practice ensures that risk management strategies are effective over time?**

- ☐ Risk identification
- ☐ Risk reduction
- ☐ Risk acceptance
- ☐ Risk monitoring

38. **Which risk management strategy involves acknowledging and living with the risk?**

- ☐ Risk avoidance
- ☐ Risk reduction
- ☐ Risk transfer
- ☐ Risk acceptance

39. **Which step involves documenting identified risks and their potential impacts?**

☐ Risk assessment
☐ Risk identification
☐ Risk communication
☐ Risk monitoring

40. **Which of the following is a key aspect of risk communication?**

☐ Identifying new risks
☐ Developing risk mitigation strategies
☐ Informing stakeholders about risks and mitigation measures
☐ Monitoring the effectiveness of risk controls

41. **What does a risk management policy typically include?**

☐ Details of financial investments
☐ Organizational structure
☐ Guidelines for risk management processes and practices
☐ Product development strategies

42. **Which process is essential for aligning risk management efforts with organizational goals?**

☐ Risk transfer
☐ Risk reduction
☐ Risk communication
☐ Risk acceptance

43. **What is the main purpose of a risk management framework?**

☐ To manage employee performance
☐ To track financial expenditures
☐ To provide a structured approach for managing risks
☐ To enhance physical security measures

44. **Which strategy involves using tools or processes to minimize risks?**

☐ Risk avoidance
☐ Risk transfer
☐ Risk reduction
☐ Risk acceptance

45. **What is the main benefit of risk transfer?**

☐ It reduces the likelihood of risks occurring
☐ It eliminates risks entirely
☐ It shifts the responsibility for managing risks to another party
☐ It minimizes the impact of risks

46. **Which risk management strategy is used when the cost of mitigating a risk is too high?**

☐ Risk avoidance
☐ Risk reduction
☐ Risk acceptance
☐ Risk transfer

47. **What is a key aspect of risk monitoring?**

☐ Identifying new risks
☐ Implementing risk controls
☐ Tracking the effectiveness of risk management strategies
☐ Training employees

48. **Which risk management practice involves adjusting strategies based on risk reviews?**

☐ Risk identification
☐ Risk assessment
☐ Risk acceptance
☐ Risk monitoring

5.7 Answers to The Questions

Great! Now, check your answers:

1. To identify, assess, and mitigate risks to protect assets

2. Risk identification

3. Risk assessment

4. Risk reduction

5. To continuously track and assess risk management effectiveness

6. Risk transfer

7. Minimizes user access to only what is necessary

8. Acknowledging a risk and deciding to live with it

9. User provisioning

10. Risk avoidance

11. To inform stakeholders about risks and mitigation strategies

12. Risk elimination

13. Risk assessment

14. Minimizing the likelihood or impact of the risk

15. Risk transfer

16. Protecting information systems from potential threats

17. Risk identification

18. Risk monitoring

19. Risk acceptance

20. Processes, policies, and procedures for managing risks

21. It ensures employees understand their roles in risk management

22. Access review and management

23. Risk avoidance

24. Risk mitigation

25. To guide risk management activities and practices

26. Risk identification

27. To minimize the likelihood or impact of a risk

28. Risk management policy

29. Risk transfer

30. Evaluating the severity and likelihood of risks

31. Risk monitoring

32. Protecting the organization's assets and objectives

33. Risk reduction

34. Implementing security controls

35. It provides a structured approach to managing risks

36. Risk assessment

37. Risk monitoring

38. Risk acceptance

39. Risk identification

40. Informing stakeholders about risks and mitigation measures

41. Guidelines for risk management processes and practices

42. Risk communication

43. To provide a structured approach for managing risks

44. Risk reduction

45. It shifts the responsibility for managing risks to another party

46. Risk acceptance

47. Tracking the effectiveness of risk management strategies

48. Risk monitoring

Chapter 6: Cybersecurity Tools and Technologies

6.1   Introduction

In the rapidly evolving field of cybersecurity, the use of specialized tools and technologies is essential for safeguarding information and systems against an array of threats. This chapter explores the fundamental tools and technologies used in cybersecurity, their functions, and their importance in maintaining robust security postures. We will cover a range of tools, from network security devices to advanced threat detection systems, and explain how they contribute to overall security strategies.

6.2   Network Security Tools

Firewalls

Firewalls are one of the primary defenses in network security, serving as barriers between trusted internal networks and untrusted external networks. They monitor and control incoming and outgoing network traffic based on predetermined security rules. Firewalls can be hardware-based, software-based, or a combination of both. Their primary function is to prevent unauthorized access and threats by enforcing security policies.

Intrusion Detection Systems (IDS) and Intrusion Prevention Systems (IPS)

Intrusion Detection Systems (IDS) are used to monitor network traffic for suspicious activities and potential threats. IDS systems generate alerts when they detect anomalies or known attack signatures. In contrast, **Intrusion Prevention Systems (IPS)** not only detect threats but also take proactive measures to prevent them from causing harm.

Both IDS and IPS are crucial for identifying and mitigating potential security breaches in real-time.

Virtual Private Networks (VPNs)

Virtual Private Networks (VPNs) provide a secure connection over the internet by encrypting data traffic and routing it through secure servers. VPNs are widely used to protect sensitive data when transmitted across public networks and to ensure privacy for remote users accessing corporate resources. They are essential for maintaining data confidentiality and integrity.

6.3   Endpoint Security Tools

Antivirus Software

Antivirus Software is designed to detect, prevent, and remove malware from individual devices. It scans files and programs for known malware signatures and suspicious behavior. Modern antivirus solutions often include additional features such as real-time protection, firewall capabilities, and email scanning to provide comprehensive endpoint protection.

Endpoint Detection and Response (EDR)

Endpoint Detection and Response (EDR) tools focus on monitoring and responding to threats that may bypass traditional antivirus solutions. EDR tools provide advanced threat detection capabilities, including behavioral analysis, forensic investigation, and automated responses to contain and remediate security incidents on endpoints.

Mobile Device Management (MDM)

Mobile Device Management (MDM) solutions are used to manage and secure mobile devices within an organization. MDM tools allow administrators to enforce security policies, remotely wipe data, and ensure compliance with organizational security standards. They are essential for protecting data on smartphones, tablets, and other mobile devices.

6.4   Threat Intelligence and Analysis Tools

Security Information and Event Management (SIEM)

Security Information and Event Management (SIEM) systems aggregate and analyze security data from various sources within an organization. SIEM solutions provide real-time visibility into security events, enabling organizations to detect and respond to threats more effectively. They offer features such as log management, correlation analysis, and alerting.

Threat Intelligence Platforms (TIPs)

Threat Intelligence Platforms (TIPs) collect and analyze data from various sources to provide insights into emerging threats and attack trends. TIPs help organizations understand the threat landscape and make informed decisions about their security posture. They often integrate with other security tools to enhance threat detection and response capabilities.

Vulnerability Management Tools

Vulnerability Management Tools are used to identify, assess, and prioritize vulnerabilities in systems and applications. These tools conduct regular scans to detect weaknesses that could be exploited by attackers. By providing actionable insights and recommendations, vulnerability management tools help organizations address security flaws and reduce their attack surface.

6.5   Data Protection Technologies

Encryption

Encryption is a fundamental technology for protecting data confidentiality and integrity. It involves converting plain text into an unreadable format using cryptographic algorithms. Encryption is used for securing data at rest, in transit, and during processing. It is crucial for protecting sensitive information from unauthorized access.

Data Loss Prevention (DLP)

Data Loss Prevention (DLP) tools are designed to prevent the unauthorized transfer or leakage of sensitive data. DLP solutions monitor and control data movement across networks and endpoints, applying policies to block or alert on potential data breaches. They are essential for protecting intellectual property and complying with data protection regulations.

Backup and Recovery Solutions

Backup and Recovery Solutions ensure that critical data can be restored in the event of a data loss incident. These solutions involve creating regular copies of data and storing them securely. Backup and recovery tools provide mechanisms for recovering data after incidents such as hardware failures, cyber-attacks, or accidental deletions.

6.6 Emerging Technologies in Cybersecurity

Artificial Intelligence (AI) and Machine Learning (ML)

Artificial Intelligence (AI) and Machine Learning (ML) are increasingly being used in cybersecurity to enhance threat detection and response. AI and ML algorithms analyze vast amounts of data to identify patterns and anomalies that may indicate malicious activity. These technologies enable more proactive and adaptive security measures.

Blockchain Technology

Blockchain Technology provides a decentralized and tamper-resistant method of recording transactions. In cybersecurity, blockchain is used for securing digital identities, ensuring data integrity, and enhancing transparency. Its inherent properties make it a promising technology for combating various types of cyber threats.

Security Automation

Security Automation involves using automated tools and processes to manage and respond to security incidents. Automation helps reduce the burden on security teams by streamlining repetitive tasks, such as log analysis, threat detection, and incident response. It enables faster and more efficient security operations.

6.7 Quiz: Technologies for Cybersecurity

1. **Which of the following tools is used to monitor network traffic for suspicious activities?**

   ☐ Antivirus Software
   ☐ Intrusion Detection System (IDS)
   ☐ Firewall
   ☐ Virtual Private Network (VPN)

2. **What is the primary function of a Virtual Private Network (VPN)?**

   ☐ To monitor and analyze network traffic
   ☐ To scan for malware
   ☐ To manage mobile devices
   ☐ To provide secure remote access and encrypt data traffic

3. **Which tool provides real-time visibility into security events by aggregating data from various sources?**

   ☐ Endpoint Detection and Response (EDR)
   ☐ Data Loss Prevention (DLP)
   ☐ Security Information and Event Management (SIEM)
   ☐ Backup and Recovery Solution

4. **Which of the following is a key feature of Endpoint Detection and Response (EDR) tools?**

   ☐ Email scanning
   ☐ Behavioral analysis and forensic investigation
   ☐ Network traffic monitoring
   ☐ Data encryption

5. **What type of tool is used to prevent unauthorized transfer of sensitive data?**

   ☐ Intrusion Prevention System (IPS)
   ☐ Virtual Private Network (VPN)
   ☐ Data Loss Prevention (DLP)
   ☐ Mobile Device Management (MDM)

6. **Which technology is used to convert plain text into unreadable**

data to protect confidentiality?

☐ Firewall
☐ Antivirus Software
☐ Encryption
☐ Backup and Recovery Solution

7. **What is the primary purpose of a firewall?**

☐ To manage mobile devices
☐ To analyze security logs
☐ To monitor and control incoming and outgoing network traffic
☐ To provide secure remote access

8. **Which tool helps in managing and securing mobile devices within an organization?**

☐ Intrusion Detection System (IDS)
☐ Data Loss Prevention (DLP)
☐ Mobile Device Management (MDM)
☐ Security Information and Event Management (SIEM)

9. **What is a primary function of Security Information and Event Management (SIEM) systems?**

☐ Aggregating and analyzing security data from various sources
☐ Encrypting data
☐ Scanning for malware
☐ Managing network traffic

10. **Which technology provides a decentralized method of recording transactions and securing digital identities?**

☐ Artificial Intelligence (AI)
☐ Encryption
☐ Virtual Private Network (VPN)
☐ Blockchain Technology

11. **Which tool is used to prevent data loss by monitoring and controlling data movement?**

☐ Endpoint Detection and Response (EDR)

- ☐ Data Loss Prevention (DLP)
- ☐ Intrusion Prevention System (IPS)
- ☐ Backup and Recovery Solution

12. **Which tool helps in restoring critical data after an incident such as hardware failure or a cyber-attack?**

- ☐ Intrusion Detection System (IDS)
- ☐ Endpoint Detection and Response (EDR)
- ☐ Data Loss Prevention (DLP)
- ☐ Backup and Recovery Solution

13. **Which technology is used to enhance threat detection and response by analyzing vast amounts of data?**

- ☐ Security Information and Event Management (SIEM)
- ☐ Artificial Intelligence (AI) and Machine Learning (ML)
- ☐ Data Loss Prevention (DLP)
- ☐ Mobile Device Management (MDM)

14. **What is the main advantage of using Security Automation?**

- ☐ Enhancing physical security measures
- ☐ Reducing cybersecurity costs
- ☐ Improving employee productivity
- ☐ Streamlining repetitive tasks and improving response efficiency

15. **Which tool is crucial for ensuring data confidentiality and integrity during transmission?**

- ☐ Virtual Private Network (VPN)
- ☐ Encryption
- ☐ Intrusion Prevention System (IPS)
- ☐ Antivirus Software

16. **Which tool focuses on monitoring endpoints for signs of suspicious activity and responding to threats?**

- ☐ Data Loss Prevention (DLP)
- ☐ Virtual Private Network (VPN)
- ☐ Mobile Device Management (MDM)

☐ Endpoint Detection and Response (EDR)

17. **Which technology allows for secure remote access and data encryption over the internet?**

   ☐ Firewall
   ☐ Intrusion Detection System (IDS)
   ☐ Virtual Private Network (VPN)
   ☐ Security Information and Event Management (SIEM)

18. **What is a key feature of Data Loss Prevention (DLP) tools?**

   ☐ Scanning for malware
   ☐ Analyzing network traffic
   ☐ Managing mobile devices
   ☐ Preventing unauthorized data transfer and leakage

19. **Which tool helps protect against unauthorized access by managing and controlling network traffic?**

   ☐ Firewall
   ☐ Mobile Device Management (MDM)
   ☐ Backup and Recovery Solution
   ☐ Threat Intelligence Platform (TIP)

20. **What is the main function of a firewall in network security?**

   ☐ To monitor and control incoming and outgoing network traffic based on security rules
   ☐ To provide secure remote access
   ☐ To scan for malware
   ☐ To manage mobile devices

21. **Which tool provides insights into emerging threats and attack trends?**

   ☐ Intrusion Detection System (IDS)
   ☐ Security Information and Event Management (SIEM)
   ☐ Endpoint Detection and Response (EDR)
   ☐ Threat Intelligence Platform (TIP)

22. **Which technology is used to manage and secure mobile devices**

in an organization?

- ☐ Data Loss Prevention (DLP)
- ☐ Encryption
- ☐ Security Information and Event Management (SIEM)
- ☐ Mobile Device Management (MDM)

23. **Which tool is designed to analyze security data and provide real-time alerts about potential threats?**

- ☐ Endpoint Detection and Response (EDR)
- ☐ Data Loss Prevention (DLP)
- ☐ Security Information and Event Management (SIEM)
- ☐ Backup and Recovery Solution

24. **What type of tool would you use to protect your organization's intellectual property from unauthorized access?**

- ☐ Data Loss Prevention (DLP)
- ☐ Virtual Private Network (VPN)
- ☐ Intrusion Detection System (IDS)
- ☐ Antivirus Software

25. **Which technology is crucial for detecting and responding to advanced threats using behavior analysis?**

- ☐ Backup and Recovery Solution
- ☐ Antivirus Software
- ☐ Data Loss Prevention (DLP)
- ☐ Endpoint Detection and Response (EDR)

26. **Which cybersecurity tool helps in managing data integrity and transparency through decentralized records?**

- ☐ Intrusion Prevention System (IPS)
- ☐ Security Information and Event Management (SIEM)
- ☐ Virtual Private Network (VPN)
- ☐ Blockchain Technology

27. **Which tool assists in monitoring and analyzing security events from different parts of an organization?**

☐ Intrusion Detection System (IDS)
☐ Security Information and Event Management (SIEM)
☐ Mobile Device Management (MDM)
☐ Data Loss Prevention (DLP)

28. **Which technology is used for securing data in transit and ensuring confidentiality?**

☐ Backup and Recovery Solution
☐ Intrusion Detection System (IDS)
☐ Endpoint Detection and Response (EDR)
☐ Encryption

29. **Which tool helps in protecting against unauthorized data leaks by monitoring data movement across networks?**

☐ Data Loss Prevention (DLP)
☐ Virtual Private Network (VPN)
☐ Security Information and Event Management (SIEM)
☐ Antivirus Software

30. **Which technology improves threat detection through the analysis of large datasets using algorithms?**

☐ Encryption
☐ Data Loss Prevention (DLP)
☐ Virtual Private Network (VPN)
☐ Artificial Intelligence (AI) and Machine Learning (ML)

31. **Which tool provides a secure and encrypted communication channel over public networks?**

☐ Data Loss Prevention (DLP)
☐ Endpoint Detection and Response (EDR)
☐ Security Information and Event Management (SIEM)
☐ Virtual Private Network (VPN)

32. **Which tool is designed to ensure that critical data can be restored after an incident?**

☐ Intrusion Prevention System (IPS)
☐ Data Loss Prevention (DLP)

☐ Mobile Device Management (MDM)
☐ Backup and Recovery Solution

33. **What type of tool would you use to protect against unauthorized access to sensitive information on endpoints?**

☐ Virtual Private Network (VPN)
☐ Backup and Recovery Solution
☐ Endpoint Detection and Response (EDR)
☐ Data Loss Prevention (DLP)

34. **Which technology enhances security by using automated processes to handle repetitive tasks?**

☐ Encryption
☐ Virtual Private Network (VPN)
☐ Security Automation
☐ Intrusion Detection System (IDS)

35. **Which tool is used to secure and monitor network traffic by applying specific security rules?**

☐ Firewall
☐ Endpoint Detection and Response (EDR)
☐ Data Loss Prevention (DLP)
☐ Intrusion Detection System (IDS)

36. **Which technology is designed to provide secure data storage and transparent transaction recording?**

☐ Security Information and Event Management (SIEM)
☐ Data Loss Prevention (DLP)
☐ Encryption
☐ Blockchain Technology

37. **Which cybersecurity tool is primarily used to prevent unauthorized network access?**

☐ Firewall
☐ Mobile Device Management (MDM)
☐ Endpoint Detection and Response (EDR)
☐ Backup and Recovery Solution

38. **Which technology helps in managing and securing mobile devices in an enterprise setting?**

- [ ] Security Information and Event Management (SIEM)
- [ ] Intrusion Detection System (IDS)
- [ ] Data Loss Prevention (DLP)
- [ ] Mobile Device Management (MDM)

39. **What is a primary use case for Data Loss Prevention (DLP) tools?**

- [ ] To manage network traffic
- [ ] To scan for malware
- [ ] To provide secure remote access
- [ ] To prevent unauthorized data leakage

40. **Which tool is used to enhance data security by ensuring that sensitive information is encrypted?**

- [ ] Data Loss Prevention (DLP)
- [ ] Mobile Device Management (MDM)
- [ ] Intrusion Detection System (IDS)
- [ ] Encryption

41. **Which technology helps in detecting and responding to threats by using machine learning algorithms?**

- [ ] Backup and Recovery Solution
- [ ] Virtual Private Network (VPN)
- [ ] Artificial Intelligence (AI) and Machine Learning (ML)
- [ ] Data Loss Prevention (DLP)

42. **Which tool is essential for managing network security and monitoring traffic for malicious activity?**

- [ ] Endpoint Detection and Response (EDR)
- [ ] Data Loss Prevention (DLP)
- [ ] Mobile Device Management (MDM)
- [ ] Firewall

43. **Which tool provides an overview of security events and logs from multiple sources?**

☐ Data Loss Prevention (DLP)
☐ Virtual Private Network (VPN)
☐ Endpoint Detection and Response (EDR)
☐ Security Information and Event Management (SIEM)

44. **Which technology allows organizations to manage their security infrastructure and automate responses?**

☐ Data Loss Prevention (DLP)
☐ Security Information and Event Management (SIEM)
☐ Mobile Device Management (MDM)
☐ Security Automation

45. **Which tool is used to protect against data breaches and unauthorized access to sensitive data?**

☐ Backup and Recovery Solution
☐ Data Loss Prevention (DLP)
☐ Intrusion Prevention System (IPS)
☐ Mobile Device Management (MDM)

46. **Which tool is essential for real-time analysis and protection of network traffic?**

☐ Data Loss Prevention (DLP)
☐ Backup and Recovery Solution
☐ Mobile Device Management (MDM)
☐ Intrusion Detection System (IDS)

47. **Which technology is used to ensure secure communications between users and the internet?**

☐ Data Loss Prevention (DLP)
☐ Endpoint Detection and Response (EDR)
☐ Backup and Recovery Solution
☐ Virtual Private Network (VPN)

48. **Which tool is used to provide insights into potential threats and help in managing network security?**

☐ Mobile Device Management (MDM)
☐ Data Loss Prevention (DLP)

☐ Security Information and Event Management (SIEM)
☐ Intrusion Detection System (IDS)

49. **Which technology provides a secure, decentralized method of recording transactions?**

☐ Data Loss Prevention (DLP)
☐ Virtual Private Network (VPN)
☐ Security Information and Event Management (SIEM)
☐ Blockchain Technology

50. **Which tool is designed to prevent unauthorized access to network resources?**

☐ Endpoint Detection and Response (EDR)
☐ Backup and Recovery Solution
☐ Data Loss Prevention (DLP)
☐ Firewall

51. **Which technology is utilized to enhance data security and manage encrypted communications?**

☐ Intrusion Prevention System (IPS)
☐ Mobile Device Management (MDM)
☐ Backup and Recovery Solution
☐ Encryption

52. **Which tool provides real-time protection against malware and other malicious threats?**

☐ Data Loss Prevention (DLP)
☐ Security Information and Event Management (SIEM)
☐ Virtual Private Network (VPN)
☐ Antivirus Software

53. **Which technology helps in the management and protection of data across different endpoints and devices?**

☐ Security Information and Event Management (SIEM)
☐ Virtual Private Network (VPN)
☐ Data Loss Prevention (DLP)
☐ Endpoint Detection and Response (EDR)

54. **Which tool helps in managing and controlling data movement across an organization's network?**

    ☐ Security Information and Event Management (SIEM)
    ☐ Intrusion Detection System (IDS)
    ☐ Backup and Recovery Solution
    ☐ Data Loss Prevention (DLP)

55. **Which tool is designed to provide a secure and encrypted connection over public networks?**

    ☐ Endpoint Detection and Response (EDR)
    ☐ Antivirus Software
    ☐ Data Loss Prevention (DLP)
    ☐ Virtual Private Network (VPN)

56. **Which technology is used to manage security incidents and automate responses to threats?**

    ☐ Security Information and Event Management (SIEM)
    ☐ Data Loss Prevention (DLP)
    ☐ Virtual Private Network (VPN)
    ☐ Security Automation

57. **Which tool provides visibility into security threats and helps in managing security events?**

    ☐ Backup and Recovery Solution
    ☐ Mobile Device Management (MDM)
    ☐ Encryption
    ☐ Security Information and Event Management (SIEM)

58. **Which tool is crucial for protecting data integrity and ensuring encrypted communication channels?**

    ☐ Intrusion Detection System (IDS)
    ☐ Data Loss Prevention (DLP)
    ☐ Mobile Device Management (MDM)
    ☐ Encryption

59. **Which tool is primarily used to analyze security events from multiple sources and provide real-time alerts?**

☐ Security Information and Event Management (SIEM)
☐ Backup and Recovery Solution
☐ Data Loss Prevention (DLP)
☐ Endpoint Detection and Response (EDR)

60. **Which technology helps in automating the detection and response to security threats?**

☐ Backup and Recovery Solution
☐ Data Loss Prevention (DLP)
☐ Virtual Private Network (VPN)
☐ Security Automation

61. **Which tool helps in the secure management of network resources and prevention of unauthorized access?**

☐ Data Loss Prevention (DLP)
☐ Mobile Device Management (MDM)
☐ Backup and Recovery Solution
☐ Firewall

62. **Which technology provides a method for managing security through decentralized and transparent records?**

☐ Intrusion Detection System (IDS)
☐ Security Information and Event Management (SIEM)
☐ Data Loss Prevention (DLP)
☐ Blockchain Technology

63. **Which tool provides protection against malware and other threats by analyzing endpoint activities?**

☐ Mobile Device Management (MDM)
☐ Backup and Recovery Solution
☐ Data Loss Prevention (DLP)
☐ Endpoint Detection and Response (EDR)

64. **Which technology is essential for ensuring secure remote access and encrypting internet traffic?**

☐ Data Loss Prevention (DLP)
☐ Endpoint Detection and Response (EDR)

☐ Intrusion Detection System (IDS)
☐ Virtual Private Network (VPN)

65. **Which tool helps protect against data breaches by monitoring and controlling sensitive data movement?**

☐ Virtual Private Network (VPN)
☐ Mobile Device Management (MDM)
☐ Data Loss Prevention (DLP)
☐ Backup and Recovery Solution

66. **Which tool is used for monitoring network traffic and identifying potential security threats?**

☐ Intrusion Detection System (IDS)
☐ Data Loss Prevention (DLP)
☐ Mobile Device Management (MDM)
☐ Endpoint Detection and Response (EDR)

67. **Which technology ensures secure communications and encrypted data exchanges over networks?**

☐ Virtual Private Network (VPN)
☐ Data Loss Prevention (DLP)
☐ Security Information and Event Management (SIEM)
☐ Encryption

68. **Which tool provides protection against threats by managing network traffic based on predefined security rules?**

☐ Firewall
☐ Endpoint Detection and Response (EDR)
☐ Data Loss Prevention (DLP)
☐ Mobile Device Management (MDM)

6.8   Answers to The Questions

Great! Now, check your answers:

1. Intrusion Detection System (IDS)

2. To provide secure remote access and encrypt data traffic

3. Security Information and Event Management (SIEM)

4. Behavioral analysis and forensic investigation

5. Data Loss Prevention (DLP)

6. Encryption

7. To monitor and control incoming and outgoing network traffic

8. Mobile Device Management (MDM)

9. Aggregating and analyzing security data from various sources

10. Blockchain Technology

11. Data Loss Prevention (DLP)

12. Backup and Recovery Solution

13. Artificial Intelligence (AI) and Machine Learning (ML)

14. Streamlining repetitive tasks and improving response efficiency

15. Encryption

16. Endpoint Detection and Response (EDR)

17. Virtual Private Network (VPN)

18. Preventing unauthorized data transfer and leakage

19. Firewall

20. To monitor and control incoming and outgoing network traffic based on security rules

21. Threat Intelligence Platform (TIP)

22. Mobile Device Management (MDM)

23. Security Information and Event Management (SIEM)

24. Data Loss Prevention (DLP)

25. Endpoint Detection and Response (EDR)

26. Blockchain Technology

27. Security Information and Event Management (SIEM)

28. Encryption

29. Data Loss Prevention (DLP)

30. Artificial Intelligence (AI) and Machine Learning (ML)

31. Virtual Private Network (VPN)

32. Backup and Recovery Solution

33. Endpoint Detection and Response (EDR)

34. Security Automation

35. Firewall

36. Blockchain Technology

37. Firewall

38. Mobile Device Management (MDM)

39. To prevent unauthorized data leakage

40. Encryption

41. Artificial Intelligence (AI) and Machine Learning (ML)

42. Firewall

43. Security Information and Event Management (SIEM)

44. Security Automation

45. Data Loss Prevention (DLP)

46. Intrusion Detection System (IDS)

47. Virtual Private Network (VPN)

48. Security Information and Event Management (SIEM)

49. Blockchain Technology

50. Firewall

51. Encryption

52. Antivirus Software

53. Endpoint Detection and Response (EDR)

54. Data Loss Prevention (DLP)

55. Virtual Private Network (VPN)

56. Security Automation

57. Security Information and Event Management (SIEM)

58. Encryption

59. Security Information and Event Management (SIEM)

60. Security Automation

61. Firewall

62. Blockchain Technology

63. Endpoint Detection and Response (EDR)

64. Virtual Private Network (VPN)

65. Data Loss Prevention (DLP)

66. Intrusion Detection System (IDS)

67. Encryption

68. Firewall

Chapter 7: How to handle Attacks and Address Vulnerabilities

7.1 Introduction

In the realm of cybersecurity, understanding threats, attacks, and vulnerabilities is essential for designing effective security measures. This chapter explores the various types of threats that organizations may encounter, the methods used in attacks, and the vulnerabilities that can be exploited. By comprehending these elements, cybersecurity professionals can better safeguard information systems and mitigate potential risks.

7.2 Understanding Threats

A threat is any potential danger that can exploit a vulnerability to cause harm to an information system. Threats can be intentional or accidental, and they come from various sources. Here, we outline the primary types of threats.

Malware

Malware, or malicious software, is designed to damage or disrupt systems. Key types of malware include:

- **Viruses:** Programs that attach themselves to legitimate files and spread to other systems.
- **Worms:** Standalone malware that replicates itself and spreads across networks.
- **Trojans:** Malicious software disguised as legitimate programs, designed to cause harm once installed.
- **Ransomware:** Encrypts a user's data and demands payment for

decryption.

Phishing

Phishing is a social engineering attack that tricks individuals into revealing sensitive information by pretending to be a trustworthy entity. Methods include:

- **Email Phishing:** Fraudulent emails that appear to come from legitimate sources.
- **Spear Phishing:** Targeted attacks aimed at specific individuals or organizations.
- **Smishing:** Phishing attempts via SMS or text messages.

Social Engineering

Social engineering exploits human psychology to gain unauthorized access. Common techniques are:

- **Pretexting:** Creating a fabricated scenario to obtain information.
- **Baiting:** Offering something enticing to lure individuals into revealing information.
- **Tailgating:** Gaining physical access by following authorized personnel.

7.3 Types of Attacks

Attacks are deliberate actions that exploit vulnerabilities. Various types include:

Denial of Service (DoS)

DoS attacks aim to make a service unavailable by overwhelming it with excessive traffic. Variants include:

- **Distributed Denial of Service (DDoS):** Uses multiple systems to flood a target.
- **Amplification Attack:** Exploits vulnerabilities to amplify the volume of attack traffic.

Man-in-the-Middle (MitM)

MitM attacks occur when an attacker intercepts and potentially alters communication between two parties. Common examples include:

- **Session Hijacking:** Stealing an active session token to gain unauthorized access.
- **Eavesdropping:** Intercepting communication without altering it.

SQL Injection

SQL injection involves inserting malicious SQL queries into input fields to manipulate a database. Key techniques include:

- **Error-Based SQL Injection:** Exploits error messages to gather information.
- **Blind SQL Injection:** Infers data based on the application's responses to crafted queries.

Cross-Site Scripting (XSS)

XSS attacks involve injecting malicious scripts into webpages. Types include:

- **Stored XSS:** Malicious scripts stored on the server and executed when the page is loaded.
- **Reflected XSS:** Scripts reflected off web servers and executed immediately.

7.4 Vulnerabilities

Vulnerabilities are weaknesses that can be exploited by threats. They can be found in software, hardware, or organizational procedures.

Software Vulnerabilities

Common software vulnerabilities include:

- **Buffer Overflow:** Occurs when more data is written to a buffer than it can handle, potentially allowing arbitrary code execution.
- **Unpatched Software:** Software missing critical updates or patches, leaving it exposed to known exploits.

- **Insecure Configuration:** Misconfigured software settings that expose systems to attacks.

Hardware Vulnerabilities

Hardware vulnerabilities can include:

- **Spectre and Meltdown:** Exploits in modern processors that allow unauthorized access to sensitive data.
- **Firmware Vulnerabilities:** Flaws in firmware that can be exploited to compromise hardware.

Organizational Vulnerabilities

These include:

- **Inadequate Policies:** Weak or non-existent security policies and procedures.
- **Lack of Training:** Insufficient training for employees on security best practices.
- **Poor Incident Response:** Ineffective processes for detecting and responding to security incidents.

7.5   Defending Against Threats and Attacks

To mitigate risks associated with threats, attacks, and vulnerabilities, organizations can employ a range of tools and strategies:

Risk Assessment and Management

Regular risk assessments help identify and prioritize threats and vulnerabilities. Risk management involves implementing controls and procedures to mitigate identified risks.

Security Tools and Technologies

Key tools include:

- **Firewalls:** Monitor and control incoming and outgoing network traffic.
- **Intrusion Detection Systems (IDS):** Detect and alert on suspicious activities.

- **Encryption:** Protect data by converting it into an unreadable format for unauthorized users.
- **Antivirus Software:** Detect and remove malware from systems.

Best Practices

Best practices for enhancing security include:

- **Regular Updates:** Keep software and systems up to date with the latest patches and updates.
- **Employee Training:** Educate employees on recognizing and responding to threats.
- **Incident Response Planning:** Develop and maintain an incident response plan to address and mitigate security incidents.

7.6 Quiz: Defend from Attacks and Address Vulnerabilities

1. What is the primary purpose of a Denial of Service (DoS) attack?

   - ☐ To gain unauthorized access
   - ☐ To steal data
   - ☐ To spread malware
   - ☐ To disrupt the availability of services

2. Which of the following best describes a Man-in-the-Middle (MitM) attack?

   - ☐ Intercepting communication between two parties
   - ☐ Overwhelming a system with traffic
   - ☐ Infecting a system with malware
   - ☐ Gaining physical access to a secure location

3. What is a common tactic used in phishing attacks?

   - ☐ Sending fraudulent emails to trick users
   - ☐ Injecting code into a website
   - ☐ Overloading a server with requests
   - ☐ Exploiting a software vulnerability

4. Which type of malware encrypts a user's data and demands payment for decryption?

   - ☐ Trojan
   - ☐ Ransomware
   - ☐ Worm
   - ☐ Spyware

5. What is a buffer overflow?

   - ☐ When more data is written to a buffer than it can handle, leading to potential code execution
   - ☐ A method of encrypting data
   - ☐ An attack that redirects users to a malicious site
   - ☐ A type of phishing attack

6. SQL injection primarily targets which of the following?

- ☐ Network firewalls
- ☐ Operating systems
- ☐ Databases
- ☐ Encryption algorithms

7. Which of the following is an example of social engineering?

- ☐ SQL injection
- ☐ Brute force attack
- ☐ Pretexting
- ☐ Zero-day exploit

8. What is cross-site scripting (XSS)?

- ☐ Injecting malicious scripts into web pages
- ☐ Overloading a system with requests
- ☐ Gaining unauthorized access to a network
- ☐ Exploiting a buffer overflow

9. Which vulnerability is often exploited in a Man-in-the-Middle (MitM) attack?

- ☐ Weak passwords
- ☐ Unpatched software
- ☐ Insecure communication channels
- ☐ Misconfigured firewalls

10. What is the main characteristic of a Trojan horse?

- ☐ It spreads by itself across networks
- ☐ It disguises itself as legitimate software
- ☐ It encrypts data for ransom
- ☐ It allows remote access to a system

11. In a Distributed Denial of Service (DDoS) attack, the attacker uses:

- ☐ A single compromised system
- ☐ Multiple compromised systems
- ☐ A phishing scam
- ☐ A SQL injection attack

12. What type of vulnerability does a SQL injection attack exploit?

- ☐ Network configuration flaws
- ☐ Web application input validation flaws
- ☐ User authentication weaknesses
- ☐ Malware on the client side

13. Which type of attack involves the attacker guessing passwords until the correct one is found?

- ☐ Brute force attack
- ☐ SQL injection
- ☐ Cross-site scripting
- ☐ Phishing

14. Which of the following describes a zero-day vulnerability?

- ☐ A vulnerability that has been patched
- ☐ A vulnerability that is unknown to the software vendor
- ☐ A weakness in physical security
- ☐ A publicly known vulnerability

15. Which attack involves tricking a user into clicking on something different from what the user perceives?

- ☐ Clickjacking
- ☐ Phishing
- ☐ SQL injection
- ☐ Cross-site scripting

16. What is the purpose of a honeypot in cybersecurity?

- ☐ To encrypt data for protection
- ☐ To lure attackers and study their methods
- ☐ To filter network traffic
- ☐ To prevent SQL injection attacks

17. Which of the following best describes a botnet?

- ☐ A type of virus that infects executable files
- ☐ A network of compromised computers controlled by an attacker

- ☐ A method for encrypting data
- ☐ A firewall configuration

18. What type of attack involves altering DNS entries to redirect users to a malicious site?

- ☐ Cross-site scripting
- ☐ DNS spoofing
- ☐ Man-in-the-Middle
- ☐ SQL injection

19. Which of the following is an example of a physical security vulnerability?

- ☐ Unpatched software
- ☐ Weak encryption algorithms
- ☐ Unlocked server room doors
- ☐ Poor password policies

20. What type of malware replicates itself to spread to other computers?

- ☐ Trojan
- ☐ Worm
- ☐ Ransomware
- ☐ Rootkit

21. Which of the following is a method to protect against phishing attacks?

- ☐ Using encryption
- ☐ Educating users to recognize phishing attempts
- ☐ Installing a firewall
- ☐ Disabling pop-up ads

22. What does the term "rootkit" refer to in cybersecurity?

- ☐ A type of firewall
- ☐ A method for encrypting data
- ☐ Malicious software that grants unauthorized root access
- ☐ A tool for network analysis

23. What is a common sign of a system infected with malware?

- ☐ Unexpected system slowdowns
- ☐ High network speeds
- ☐ Enhanced security features
- ☐ Regular system updates

24. Which of the following is a method for securing web applications from cross-site scripting (XSS) attacks?

- ☐ Disabling JavaScript
- ☐ Validating and sanitizing user input
- ☐ Using a VPN
- ☐ Encrypting network traffic

25. What is the primary function of a firewall in network security?

- ☐ To filter incoming and outgoing network traffic
- ☐ To encrypt data
- ☐ To detect malware
- ☐ To monitor network performance

26. Which of the following can be classified as an insider threat?

- ☐ A disgruntled employee leaking confidential information
- ☐ A hacker gaining access through a vulnerability
- ☐ A phishing attack targeting employees
- ☐ A worm spreading across the network

27. Which of the following is a common indicator of a phishing email?

- ☐ The email is encrypted
- ☐ The email is from a known contact
- ☐ The email contains urgent or threatening language
- ☐ The email has no attachments

28. Which attack targets users by exploiting vulnerabilities in their web browser?

- ☐ Phishing
- ☐ Drive-by download
- ☐ SQL injection
- ☐ Denial of Service (DoS)

29. What type of attack involves an attacker trying all possible combinations of a password?

- ☐ Brute force attack
- ☐ Social engineering
- ☐ SQL injection
- ☐ Cross-site scripting

30. Which of the following describes a privilege escalation attack?

- ☐ Accessing a network without authorization
- ☐ Gaining elevated access rights to perform unauthorized actions
- ☐ Disrupting services by overwhelming them with traffic
- ☐ Exploiting vulnerabilities in encryption algorithms

31. Which of the following best describes a logic bomb?

- ☐ A type of phishing attack
- ☐ A virus that spreads through email
- ☐ Malicious code that triggers under certain conditions
- ☐ A method for cracking passwords

32. What is a common feature of ransomware?

- ☐ It deletes system files
- ☐ It encrypts data and demands payment
- ☐ It spreads through USB drives
- ☐ It provides unauthorized remote access

33. Which of the following is an effective method for protecting against brute force attacks?

- ☐ Disabling pop-ups
- ☐ Implementing account lockout policies
- ☐ Using encryption
- ☐ Conducting regular software updates

34. What is the main objective of a phishing attack?

- ☐ To damage hardware
- ☐ To disrupt services

- ☐ To steal sensitive information
- ☐ To create a backdoor for future attacks

35. Which of the following best describes an Advanced Persistent Threat (APT)?

  - ☐ A short-term attack with immediate impact
  - ☐ A simple attack targeting small businesses
  - ☐ A prolonged, targeted attack by a skilled adversary
  - ☐ A physical attack on infrastructure

36. What is the purpose of a patch in the context of cybersecurity?

  - ☐ To fix vulnerabilities in software
  - ☐ To encrypt data
  - ☐ To monitor network traffic
  - ☐ To create backup copies of files

37. Which of the following is a key characteristic of a worm?

  - ☐ It replicates and spreads independently
  - ☐ It requires user interaction to spread
  - ☐ It encrypts files for ransom
  - ☐ It logs keystrokes to steal information

38. Which of the following methods is commonly used to detect vulnerabilities in a system?

  - ☐ Encryption
  - ☐ Social engineering
  - ☐ Vulnerability scanning
  - ☐ Phishing

39. What is the main function of a rootkit in a compromised system?

  - ☐ To encrypt files for ransom
  - ☐ To spread across networks
  - ☐ To hide the presence of malicious activities
  - ☐ To inject code into websites

7.7 Answer to The Questions

Great! Now, check your answers:

1. To disrupt the availability of services

2. Intercepting communication between two parties

3. Sending fraudulent emails to trick users

4. Ransomware

5. When more data is written to a buffer than it can handle, leading to potential code execution

6. Databases

7. Pretexting

8. Injecting malicious scripts into web pages

9. Insecure communication channels

10. It disguises itself as legitimate software

11. Multiple compromised systems

12. Web application input validation flaws

13. Brute force attack

14. A vulnerability that is unknown to the software vendor

15. Clickjacking

16. To lure attackers and study their methods

17. A network of compromised computers controlled by an attacker

18. DNS spoofing

19. Unlocked server room doors

20. Worm

21. Educating users to recognize phishing attempts

22. Malicious software that grants unauthorized root access

23. Unexpected system slowdowns

24. Validating and sanitizing user input

25. To filter incoming and outgoing network traffic

26. A disgruntled employee leaking confidential information

27. The email contains urgent or threatening language

28. Drive-by download

29. Brute force attack

30. Gaining elevated access rights to perform unauthorized actions

31. Malicious code that triggers under certain conditions

32. It encrypts data and demands payment

33. Implementing account lockout policies

34. To steal sensitive information

35. A prolonged, targeted attack by a skilled adversary

36. To fix vulnerabilities in software

37. It replicates and spreads independently

38. Vulnerability scanning

39. To hide the presence of malicious activities

Chapter 8: Cloud Infrastructures and Cloud Security

8.1 Introduction to Cloud Computing

Cloud computing has transformed how businesses and individuals store, manage, and access data. By leveraging remote servers hosted on the internet, organizations can reduce costs, increase efficiency, and scale operations more effectively. This chapter delves into the fundamental concepts of cloud infrastructures and the security considerations essential for safeguarding cloud environments.

8.2 Types of Cloud Models

Cloud computing is categorized into different models based on deployment and service offerings. Understanding these models is crucial for organizations to choose the right cloud solution that aligns with their needs.

Public Cloud

A public cloud is owned and operated by third-party cloud service providers, delivering computing resources such as servers and storage over the internet. Examples include Amazon Web Services (AWS), Microsoft Azure, and Google Cloud Platform. Public clouds offer scalability and flexibility but pose significant security challenges due to their shared infrastructure.

Private Cloud

A private cloud is dedicated to a single organization, offering more control over the infrastructure and data. It can be hosted on-premises or by a third-party provider. Private clouds are preferred by organizations that require high security, regulatory compliance, and customizability.

Hybrid Cloud

Hybrid cloud combines elements of both public and private clouds, allowing data and applications to be shared between them. This model offers greater flexibility and optimized existing infrastructure investments. Organizations often use hybrid clouds to manage sensitive data in private clouds while leveraging the public cloud for less critical operations.

8.3   Cloud Service Models

Cloud services are categorized into three primary models, each offering different levels of control, flexibility, and management responsibilities.

Infrastructure as a Service (IaaS)

IaaS provides virtualized computing resources over the internet, including virtual machines, storage, and networks. It allows businesses to rent IT infrastructure on a pay-as-you-go basis, reducing the need for on-premises hardware. Examples include AWS EC2 and Google Compute Engine.

Platform as a Service (PaaS)

PaaS offers a platform for developers to build, deploy, and manage applications without dealing with the underlying infrastructure. It includes development tools, databases, and middleware. PaaS simplifies the development process but requires trust in the platform provider's security measures. Examples include Microsoft Azure App Services and Google App Engine.

Software as a Service (SaaS)

SaaS delivers software applications over the internet, typically on a subscription basis. Users access the software through a web browser, with the provider managing the infrastructure, middleware, and application data. Examples include Salesforce, Microsoft Office 365, and Google Workspace.

8.4 Cloud Security Challenges

As organizations migrate to the cloud, they face several security challenges that must be addressed to protect sensitive data and ensure compliance with regulations.

Data Security and Privacy

Data stored in the cloud is often subject to different regulations depending on the geographical location of the data centers. Organizations must ensure that data is encrypted both at rest and in transit, and access is strictly controlled. Data breaches in the cloud can lead to significant financial and reputational damage.

Identity and Access Management (IAM)

Managing who has access to cloud resources is critical. IAM involves policies and technologies that control user access to sensitive information. Multi-factor authentication (MFA), role-based access control (RBAC), and least privilege principles are essential components of a robust IAM strategy in the cloud.

Shared Responsibility Model

In cloud environments, security responsibilities are shared between the cloud provider and the customer. While providers secure the infrastructure, customers are responsible for securing their data, applications, and user access. Understanding this model is crucial for effective cloud security management.

8.5 Securing Cloud Infrastructures

To mitigate the risks associated with cloud computing, organizations must implement robust security measures tailored to their specific cloud environment.

Encryption

Encryption is a critical component of cloud security, ensuring that data is unreadable to unauthorized users. Organizations should use strong encryption methods for data at rest, in transit, and during processing.

Key management is also a vital consideration, as improper handling of encryption keys can compromise data security.

Network Security

Securing the network layer is essential in cloud environments to prevent unauthorized access and attacks. This includes implementing firewalls, intrusion detection and prevention systems (IDPS), and virtual private networks (VPNs). Segmentation of networks in the cloud can also help limit the spread of malware or attacks within an organization's infrastructure.

Monitoring and Incident Response

Continuous monitoring of cloud environments is necessary to detect and respond to security incidents promptly. Organizations should implement security information and event management (SIEM) systems to collect and analyze security data. Having an incident response plan tailored to the cloud environment ensures quick and effective action in the event of a breach.

8.6   Compliance and Regulatory Considerations

Organizations must navigate a complex landscape of regulations and standards when operating in the cloud. Compliance with industry-specific regulations, such as GDPR for data protection or HIPAA for healthcare, is critical.

Data Sovereignty

Data sovereignty refers to the legal implications of storing data in different jurisdictions. Organizations must be aware of where their data is stored and ensure compliance with local laws, which may require data to be stored within the borders of a specific country.

Auditing and Certification

Regular audits of cloud environments help ensure compliance with security standards and regulations. Many cloud providers offer certifications that demonstrate their adherence to security practices, such as ISO 27001 or SOC 2. These certifications provide assurance to customers that the cloud provider meets specific security benchmarks.

8.7 Best Practices for Cloud Security

Implementing best practices for cloud security helps organizations minimize risks and protect their assets.

Adopt a Zero Trust Model

The Zero Trust security model assumes that threats exist both inside and outside the network. In a cloud environment, this means continuously verifying user identities, enforcing least privilege access, and monitoring all activity.

Regular Security Assessments

Conducting regular security assessments and vulnerability scans in the cloud environment helps identify potential weaknesses before they can be exploited. These assessments should include penetration testing, configuration reviews, and compliance audits.

Training and Awareness

Educating employees about cloud security risks and best practices is essential. Regular training ensures that all staff members understand their role in maintaining the security of cloud systems and data.

8.8 Emerging Trends in Cloud Security

As cloud computing evolves, new security challenges and technologies emerge. Staying informed about these trends is crucial for maintaining robust cloud security.

AI and Machine Learning in Cloud Security

Artificial intelligence (AI) and machine learning (ML) are increasingly used to enhance cloud security. These technologies can analyze vast amounts of data to identify patterns, detect anomalies, and respond to threats faster than traditional methods.

8.9 Quiz: Cloud Infrastructure and Cloud Security

1. What is the main benefit of using a public cloud service?

   - ☐ Greater control over hardware
   - ☐ Scalability and cost-efficiency
   - ☐ Increased physical security
   - ☐ Customized hardware configurations

2. Which cloud service model provides the most control over the underlying infrastructure?

   - ☐ Software as a Service (SaaS)
   - ☐ Platform as a Service (PaaS)
   - ☐ Infrastructure as a Service (IaaS)
   - ☐ Storage as a Service (STaaS)

3. In a hybrid cloud environment, what is the primary advantage of integrating both public and private clouds?

   - ☐ Increased physical security
   - ☐ Reduced cost of cloud services
   - ☐ Greater flexibility and optimization of existing infrastructure
   - ☐ Improved vendor support

4. What does the Shared Responsibility Model in cloud security imply?

   - ☐ The cloud provider is responsible for all security measures.
   - ☐ The customer is responsible for managing hardware.
   - ☐ Security responsibilities are divided between the cloud provider and the customer.
   - ☐ Both parties share the responsibility for compliance only.

5. Which of the following is a key feature of Cloud-Native security tools?

   - ☐ They are designed for on-premises environments.
   - ☐ They require extensive hardware resources.

- ☐ They integrate seamlessly with cloud services.
- ☐ They are generally less scalable than traditional tools.

6. What is a common security concern associated with SaaS applications?

   - ☐ Physical hardware tampering
   - ☐ Poor scalability options
   - ☐ Data privacy and control over data stored in the cloud
   - ☐ High costs of infrastructure

7. Which principle is essential for securing data in the cloud?

   - ☐ Relying solely on the cloud provider's security
   - ☐ Implementing strong encryption for data at rest and in transit
   - ☐ Avoiding the use of multi-factor authentication
   - ☐ Disabling logging and monitoring

8. What does the Zero Trust model entail for cloud security?

   - ☐ Trusting all users inside the network
   - ☐ Continuously verifying user identities and enforcing least privilege
   - ☐ Allowing unrestricted access to cloud resources
   - ☐ Relying solely on perimeter defenses

9. Why is multi-factor authentication (MFA) important in cloud environments?

   - ☐ It simplifies user login processes.
   - ☐ It reduces the number of passwords required.
   - ☐ It adds an additional layer of security beyond just passwords.
   - ☐ It prevents data encryption needs.

10. Which cloud service model would be most suitable for a developer needing to build and deploy applications without managing the underlying infrastructure?

    - ☐ Infrastructure as a Service (IaaS)
    - ☐ Software as a Service (SaaS)

- ☐ Platform as a Service (PaaS)
- ☐ Network as a Service (NaaS)

11. What is the main focus of data sovereignty in cloud computing?

- ☐ Increasing data access speed
- ☐ Compliance with legal and regulatory requirements based on data location
- ☐ Enhancing system performance
- ☐ Simplifying data management

12. Which of the following is a benefit of using a private cloud?

- ☐ Lower overall cost than public cloud options
- ☐ Greater control over security and compliance
- ☐ Automatic scaling of resources
- ☐ Simplified vendor management

13. How does encryption contribute to cloud security?

- ☐ By improving network speed
- ☐ By making data unreadable to unauthorized users
- ☐ By reducing storage costs
- ☐ By simplifying user access management

14. What is a key characteristic of a hybrid cloud deployment?

- ☐ Complete separation of public and private resources
- ☐ Integration and coordination between public and private clouds
- ☐ Only using public cloud services
- ☐ Exclusive use of on-premises infrastructure

15. Which of the following best describes a cloud security incident response plan?

- ☐ A procedure for hardware maintenance
- ☐ A set of actions to detect, respond to, and recover from security incidents in the cloud
- ☐ A guideline for software development
- ☐ A plan for reducing cloud service costs

16. What is the role of security information and event management (SIEM) in cloud security?

- ☐ Enhancing physical security
- ☐ Aggregating and analyzing security data to detect and respond to threats
- ☐ Managing cloud service costs
- ☐ Simplifying cloud resource provisioning

17. How can organizations ensure compliance with cloud security regulations?

- ☐ By ignoring certification requirements
- ☐ By regularly conducting audits and adhering to industry certifications
- ☐ By limiting data encryption
- ☐ By avoiding security monitoring tools

18. What is a key feature of cloud-native security tools compared to traditional tools?

- ☐ They require significant on-premises infrastructure
- ☐ They are designed for use in on-premises environments
- ☐ They are optimized for integration with cloud services and scalability
- ☐ They offer less automation

19. Which approach helps in protecting sensitive data in cloud environments?

- ☐ Using only basic passwords
- ☐ Implementing strong encryption and access controls
- ☐ Relying solely on network security
- ☐ Avoiding the use of data backups

20. How can cloud security be enhanced through network configuration?

- ☐ By allowing unrestricted access to all network segments
- ☐ By implementing network segmentation and access controls
- ☐ By reducing the number of firewalls
- ☐ By disabling logging and monitoring

21. What is the main purpose of multi-factor authentication (MFA) in cloud security?

- ☐ To make login processes simpler
- ☐ To reduce the need for complex passwords
- ☐ To provide an additional layer of security beyond passwords
- ☐ To improve network performance

22. What does the term "data residency" refer to in cloud computing?

- ☐ The geographic location where data is stored
- ☐ The regulations and legal requirements associated with data storage location
- ☐ The process of data encryption
- ☐ The method of data backup

23. Which of the following is NOT a characteristic of a public cloud?

- ☐ Dedicated resources for a single organization
- ☐ Shared resources with multiple tenants
- ☐ Pay-as-you-go pricing
- ☐ Scalability

24. What is the main benefit of using encryption for data in transit?

- ☐ Improved data compression
- ☐ Enhanced system performance
- ☐ Protection against interception and unauthorized access during transmission
- ☐ Simplified data storage management

25. How does the Zero Trust model improve cloud security?

- ☐ By trusting all users inside the network
- ☐ By continuously verifying and validating user and device identities
- ☐ By allowing unrestricted access to cloud resources
- ☐ By focusing only on perimeter security

26. What is a cloud access security broker (CASB) used for?

- ☐ To manage cloud service contracts

- ☐ To enforce security policies and monitor access to cloud services
- ☐ To provide physical security for data centers
- ☐ To reduce cloud service costs

27. What does the term "cloud bursting" refer to?

- ☐ A method for reducing cloud service costs
- ☐ The process of extending private cloud capacity to a public cloud during high demand
- ☐ A technique for encrypting data
- ☐ A way to improve network performance

28. Which of the following is a benefit of using containerization in cloud environments?

- ☐ Increased reliance on traditional virtual machines
- ☐ Consistent and efficient deployment of applications across different environments
- ☐ Higher hardware resource consumption
- ☐ Reduced scalability

29. What is the primary purpose of a cloud security posture management (CSPM) tool?

- ☐ To manage cloud service costs
- ☐ To continuously monitor and improve cloud security configurations and compliance
- ☐ To provide physical security for cloud data centers
- ☐ To simplify cloud service provisioning

30. What role does a cloud service provider's Service Level Agreement (SLA) play in cloud security?

- ☐ It defines the cost of cloud services
- ☐ It outlines the security responsibilities and guarantees provided by the cloud service provider
- ☐ It specifies the physical location of data centers
- ☐ It determines the hardware specifications for cloud services

31. How does a virtual private cloud (VPC) enhance cloud security?

- ☐ By increasing the physical security of data centers
- ☐ By creating a logically isolated section of the cloud for enhanced control and security
- ☐ By providing unrestricted access to cloud resources
- ☐ By reducing data encryption needs

32. What is a common method for ensuring data integrity in cloud environments?

- ☐ Relying solely on cloud service provider security measures
- ☐ Implementing hash functions and digital signatures
- ☐ Disabling encryption
- ☐ Reducing data backups

33. How can organizations manage access controls effectively in a cloud environment?

- ☐ By avoiding the use of role-based access control
- ☐ By implementing strong identity and access management policies and practices
- ☐ By limiting the use of multi-factor authentication
- ☐ By ignoring least privilege principles

34. What is a significant security consideration when using cloud storage services?

- ☐ The need for more physical storage space
- ☐ Ensuring proper encryption and access controls for stored data
- ☐ Increased reliance on local backups
- ☐ Higher costs for data retrieval

35. Which cloud deployment model offers the most control and customization for an organization?

- ☐ Public cloud
- ☐ Private cloud
- ☐ Community cloud
- ☐ Hybrid cloud

36. What is the purpose of a cloud security incident response plan?

- ☐ To manage cloud service costs
- ☐ To establish procedures for detecting, responding to, and recovering from security incidents in the cloud
- ☐ To enhance cloud service performance
- ☐ To simplify cloud resource management

37. Which of the following is a common cloud security best practice?

- ☐ Avoiding the use of encryption
- ☐ Regularly updating and patching cloud services
- ☐ Ignoring access controls
- ☐ Disabling monitoring tools

38. What is the primary benefit of using a cloud-native security approach?

- ☐ It provides fewer security features than traditional tools.
- ☐ It requires more manual configuration.
- ☐ It offers integrated and automated security features optimized for cloud environments.
- ☐ It limits scalability.

39. How can organizations ensure that their cloud applications are secure from vulnerabilities?

- ☐ By avoiding regular vulnerability assessments
- ☐ By conducting regular security assessments and applying security patches
- ☐ By disabling automatic updates
- ☐ By relying solely on the cloud provider's security measures

40. What is a key benefit of using cloud security monitoring tools?

- ☐ They reduce the need for data encryption.
- ☐ They provide real-time visibility into security events and potential threats.
- ☐ They simplify user authentication.
- ☐ They manage cloud service costs.

41. What does the term "cloud security posture management" refer to?

- ☐ Managing physical security of cloud data centers

- ☐ Continuously assessing and improving security configurations and compliance in the cloud
- ☐ Handling cloud service provider contracts
- ☐ Reducing data storage needs

42. Which of the following is a key factor in selecting a cloud service provider?

- ☐ The provider's hardware specifications
- ☐ The provider's security features and compliance with industry standards
- ☐ The physical location of the data centers
- ☐ The provider's software development practices

43. How does a cloud provider's Service Level Agreement (SLA) impact security?

- ☐ It defines the cost of services.
- ☐ It specifies the security measures and responsibilities of the provider.
- ☐ It outlines the physical location of data centers.
- ☐ It determines the hardware specifications for cloud services.

44. What is a cloud security vulnerability assessment used for?

- ☐ To enhance data storage capabilities
- ☐ To identify and address potential security weaknesses in cloud systems
- ☐ To increase network bandwidth
- ☐ To simplify cloud service management

45. What role does a cloud access security broker (CASB) play in cloud security?

- ☐ It provides physical security for data centers.
- ☐ It helps enforce security policies and monitor access to cloud services.
- ☐ It manages cloud service contracts.
- ☐ It simplifies cloud resource provisioning.

46. What is the primary purpose of implementing strong encryption in cloud environments?

- □ To reduce data retrieval times
- □ To lower storage costs
- □ To protect data from unauthorized access and breaches
- □ To simplify data backups

47. How can organizations mitigate risks associated with cloud computing?

    - □ By avoiding the use of multi-factor authentication
    - □ By implementing comprehensive security policies, encryption, and regular assessments
    - □ By ignoring data encryption needs
    - □ By limiting access to cloud services

48. What is a key characteristic of a cloud-native security tool?

    - □ It is designed for on-premises environments.
    - □ It requires extensive manual configuration.
    - □ It integrates seamlessly with cloud services and scales with cloud environments.
    - □ It has limited automation features.

49. Which of the following best describes the concept of "data isolation" in cloud computing?

    - □ Sharing data across multiple organizations
    - □ Consolidating all data in a single location
    - □ Ensuring that data from different clients or tenants remains separate and secure
    - □ Disabling access controls

50. How can organizations enhance their cloud security posture?

    - □ By avoiding regular security updates
    - □ By adopting a proactive security strategy that includes monitoring, encryption, and compliance measures
    - □ By relying solely on cloud provider security
    - □ By reducing data encryption

8.10 Answers to The Questions

Great! Now, check your answers:

1. Scalability and cost-efficiency

2. Infrastructure as a Service (IaaS)

3. Greater flexibility and optimization of existing infrastructure

4. Security responsibilities are divided between the cloud provider and the customer.

5. They integrate seamlessly with cloud services.

6. Data privacy and control over data stored in the cloud

7. Implementing strong encryption for data at rest and in transit

8. Continuously verifying user identities and enforcing least privilege

9. It adds an additional layer of security beyond just passwords.

10. Platform as a Service (PaaS)

11. Compliance with legal and regulatory requirements based on data location

12. Greater control over security and compliance

13. By making data unreadable to unauthorized users

14. Integration and coordination between public and private clouds

15. A set of actions to detect, respond to, and recover from security incidents in the cloud

16. Aggregating and analyzing security data to detect and respond to threats

17. By regularly conducting audits and adhering to industry certifications

18. They are optimized for integration with cloud services and scalability

19. Implementing strong encryption and access controls

20. By implementing network segmentation and access controls

21. To provide an additional layer of security beyond passwords

22. The regulations and legal requirements associated with

data storage location

23. Shared resources with multiple tenants

24. Protection against interception and unauthorized access during transmission

25. By continuously verifying and validating user and device identities

26. To enforce security policies and monitor access to cloud services

27. The process of extending private cloud capacity to a public cloud during high demand

28. Consistent and efficient deployment of applications across different environments

29. To continuously monitor and improve cloud security configurations and compliance

30. It outlines the security responsibilities and guarantees provided by the cloud service provider

31. By creating a logically isolated section of the cloud for enhanced control and security

32. Implementing hash functions

and digital signatures

33. By implementing strong identity and access management policies and practices

34. Ensuring proper encryption and access controls for stored data

35. Private cloud

36. To establish procedures for detecting, responding to, and recovering from security incidents in the cloud

37. Regularly updating and patching cloud services

38. It offers integrated and automated security features optimized for cloud environments.

39. By conducting regular security assessments and applying security patches

40. They provide real-time visibility into security events and potential threats.

41. Continuously assessing and improving security configurations and compliance in the cloud

42. The provider's security features and compliance with industry standards

43. It specifies the security measures and responsibilities of the provider.

44. To identify and address potential security weaknesses in cloud systems

45. It helps enforce security policies and monitor access to cloud services.

46. To protect data from unauthorized access and breaches

47. By implementing comprehensive security policies, encryption, and regular assessments

48. It integrates seamlessly with cloud services and scales with cloud environments.

49. Ensuring that data from different clients or tenants remains separate and secure

50. By adopting a proactive security strategy that includes monitoring, encryption, and

Bonus Chapter: Exam Preparation and Strategies

Preparing for the CompTIA Security+ exam requires a thorough understanding of the exam content and effective strategies to maximize your chances of success. This chapter provides detailed guidance on how to prepare effectively for the exam, including study techniques, resources, and test-taking strategies.

9.1   Understanding the Exam Format

The CompTIA Security+ exam is designed to assess your knowledge and skills in cybersecurity. The exam format typically includes multiple-choice questions, as well as performance-based questions (PBQs) that test your ability to apply your knowledge in practical scenarios.

Multiple-Choice Questions

Multiple-choice questions (MCQs) are the most common type of questions on the Security+ exam. These questions may have one or more correct answers. Understanding the question thoroughly and carefully considering all options is essential. Practice answering MCQs under timed conditions to simulate the exam environment.

Performance-Based Questions (PBQs)

Performance-based questions require you to solve practical problems or complete tasks related to cybersecurity scenarios. These questions test your ability to apply theoretical knowledge in real-world situations. Familiarize yourself with common PBQ formats and practice using simulation tools to build your skills.

9.2 Effective Study Techniques

Developing an effective study plan is crucial for success on the Security+ exam. Here are some strategies to help you prepare:

Create a Study Plan

Start by creating a study plan that outlines your study goals, timeline, and resources. Allocate specific time each day for studying and stick to your plan. Divide your study sessions into manageable chunks, focusing on different topics each time.

Utilize Study Resources

Leverage a variety of study resources, including textbooks, online courses, practice exams, and study guides. The CompTIA Security+ study guide and practice tests are valuable tools that can help you become familiar with the exam content and question formats.

Join Study Groups

Joining a study group can provide additional support and motivation. Study groups allow you to discuss topics, ask questions, and share knowledge with others who are also preparing for the exam. Engaging with peers can help reinforce your understanding of complex concepts.

9.3 Test-Taking Strategies

Effective test-taking strategies can help you perform better on exam day. Here are some tips to keep in mind:

Read Questions Carefully

Carefully read each question and all answer choices before selecting your response. Pay attention to keywords and phrases that indicate what the question is asking. Avoid rushing through questions, as this can lead to mistakes.

Manage Your Time

Time management is crucial during the exam. Allocate a specific amount of time to each question and move on if you encounter a difficult one. If you have time remaining, review your answers and make any necessary corrections.

Use the Process of Elimination

If you are unsure about an answer, use the process of elimination to narrow down your options. Eliminate clearly incorrect choices to improve your chances of selecting the correct answer from the remaining options.

9.4 Review and Practice

Regular review and practice are key to reinforcing your knowledge and improving your exam performance.

Take Practice Exams

Regularly taking practice exams will help you become familiar with the exam format and question types. Practice exams also allow you to assess your readiness and identify areas where you need additional study.

Review Incorrect Answers

Review your practice exam results to understand any mistakes you made. Analyzing incorrect answers can help you identify knowledge gaps and improve your understanding of the material.

Stay Updated

Cybersecurity is a constantly evolving field. Stay updated with the latest developments and changes in the industry. Review any recent updates to the exam objectives and ensure that your study materials are current.

9.5 On Exam Day

Preparing for exam day is just as important as your study efforts. Here are some final tips for exam day:

Get Adequate Rest

Ensure you get a good night's sleep before the exam. Being well-rested will help you stay focused and perform better.

Arrive Early

Arrive at the testing center early to allow time for check-in and to get settled before the exam begins. This will help reduce any pre-exam stress.

Follow Exam Instructions

Follow all instructions provided by the exam proctor. Ensure you understand the rules and procedures for taking the exam, including how to handle breaks and submit your answers.

By following these strategies and thoroughly preparing, you can increase your chances of passing the CompTIA Security+ exam and achieving your certification goals. Good luck with your preparation and the exam!

Always remember that passing the exam is your solely responsibility and you must put all your effort and concentration in this purpose before, during and even after executing it!

www.ingramcontent.com/pod-product-compliance
Lightning Source LLC
LaVergne TN
LVHW051234050326
832903LV00028B/2397